Contents

Prolegomena

Julius Lipner

On January 1st, 1995, the Dharam Hinduja Institute of Indic Research was established, for five years in the first instance, in the Centre for Advanced Religious and Theological Studies of the Divinity Faculty of Cambridge University, through a generous benefaction of the Hinduja Foundation (UK). The aim of the Institute is to study the Indic traditions, with a special focus on Hinduism, in an interdisciplinary context and with the practical relevance and public outreach of this research in view. The Inaugural Conference of the Institute was held on June 30th – July 1st, 1995, under the title that appears on this book. The Conference was a highly successful international event with packed attendances of scholars, research students and people from various professional and other walks of life. At the end of the Conference it was decided that the various papers, understandably presented somewhat informally during the event, be formulated in a more considered manner and published. We are very glad to be doing so.[1]

There are a number of reasons why the present theme was chosen for the Inaugural Conference: these reasons have to do with their bearing on a tradition that is a prime focus of the Institute, and on a text with an established history that has played and continues to play a most significant role in the lives not only of countless individuals but also of a great many communities, a text which raises acutely questions of interpretation and the transmission of knowledge, of the relevance of meaning and the determining of right action, of personal commitment in contrast to "objective study", of barriers — and their possible overcoming — of culture and approach, in short, "questions about intentions, foundations, boundaries, knowledge and power" (Hirst, p. 49). The *Gītā* is a challenging text if ever there was one.

There is a criterial pusillanimity, a methodological loss of nerve, in much of western scholarship today. This pivots on what has been called the historical-critical method, which is supposed to be "objective", i.e. emotionally dispassionate, epistemologically neutral, and uni-disciplinary, in contrast to "subjective" approaches that function through the agency of personal faiths and commitments of one kind or another. For want of a viable substitute, I am not opposed to the use of "objective" to characterise academic study. I am deeply opposed, however, to its uncritical endorsement, and to the seductive and errant virus of absolutism it so insidiously implants in the mind of the scholar. It obscures the fact, which scholarship based on another *modus operandi,* emerging from such contexts as the "liberation subjects" (e.g. feminism, liberation theology, environmental and ecological studies), has begun to alert us to, viz. that the boundary between "objective" and "subjective" as distinguished above is systematically elusive and methodologically blurred — that, in short, the "objective" scholar inevitably, indeed constitutionally, brings a host of "subjective" *selective* criteria to bear in pursuit of his or her professional work, such as one's particular academic conditioning, temperament and personal prejudices, and the current political environment in which one must function (think of the corrective *and* distortive effects of political correctness). These guiding and constitutive criteria of "objective" scholarship are expressions of faiths/personal commitments too, and affect the form and content of one's conclusions.

The solution then is not to make facile distinctions between "objective" and "subjective" approaches, but to engage instead in psychological archeology, viz. unearthing in a systematic and informed manner the selective personal factors underlying one's academic approach and expertise, acknowledging these (at least to oneself), and then *compensating* for them academically. This introduces a healthy relativism in one's professional work; it reduces opinionatedness and creates a "doctrinal tolerance", viz. an awareness that one's own conclusions may be valid so far as they go, but that they are not likely to go far enough; that they are not necessarily comprehensive, or even definitive, and that their fragmentary and temporary nature is inherently susceptible to revision in the light of further knowledge and to reinterpretation in the context of larger wholes or reconstructed perspectives. In short, by dying continually through a thousand qualifications, these conclusions are reborn continually through those very qualifications.

This approach then must accommodate the view that a text, especially a living religious text like the *Bhagavadgītā*, is a multi-layered product: the legitimate object of study for the professional theologian no less than for the Indologist, indeed, for the theological Indologist no less than for the philologist, and that it is an object of faith as well as an object of research. A full appreciation of a text like the *Gītā* must be an integrated one, and notwithstanding the drawing of legitimate distinctions of approach, e.g. the theological as distinct from the philological, the scholar must be prepared to acknowledge that any uni-disciplinary approach is but partial and cannot begin to do justice to such an object of study.

It was for this most legitimate of academic reasons then that a professional (Christian) theologian was asked to produce the keynote address of the Conference and the first essay in this book. As is obvious, Professor Lash has subjected the *Gītā* to careful analytical scrutiny. The result is a penetrating and fascinating study. What does the *Gītā* — that most vaunted of Hindu texts — have to say to a culturally and methodologically sensitive Christian theologian, and what light can that theologian shed, in turn, for the Indologist, irrespective of the latter's particular specialism?

Unerringly, Lash sought out the pith (*sāra*) of *Gītā* teaching: it has to do with the ethics (the *dharma)* of desire, for as Brockington points out in his immensely learned essay, "the *Bhagavadgītā*.....declares that, since desire is more basic than action, actions as such have no particular effect, provided one acts unselfishly and without interest in the result" (p. 37-38), that is, unselfish actions have no particular effect on one's karma provided one acts in accordance with *dharma.* [2]

Lash entitles his contribution, "The Purification of Desire". The title is significant: it encapsulates his conclusions on a key issue he raises — Granted that the *Gītā* is concerned basically with the ethics of desire, does it recommend the *purification* of desire or its *suppression*? Ethically, surely this is a burning question for our times, for its answer will generate not only a particular worldview, but a code of conduct arising from it. The contours of a life based on "the cleansing of desire" are very different from one based on its "abolition" (Lash, p.3)

A number of the contributors have pointed to the seeming ambivalence of the text on this question, as does Lash. On the one hand, the ethics of sacrifice and asceticism has a high profile in the *Gītā*.[3] In traditional Brahminical Hinduism, this was an ethics that favoured the suppression of desire. Here, everyday desire is inherently tainted with egoism and self-interest — the sphere of the I-maker *(ahaṃkāra)* — characterised by a hankering for the gratifying fruits of one's actions. Nothing short of its ruthless extirpation will produce the conditions necessary for living the ideal life, a life weighted maximally towards a self-absorbing discipline of contemplation on the dispassionate core of one's being, the *ātman,* and minimally towards action of any kind; only this course would dissolve past karma and lead to a cessation of rebirth from a cycle of life that is characterised as an abode of sorrow (*duḥkhālayam, Gītā* 8.15).[4]

In his essay, Gavin Flood has shown how key elements of this Hindu ideal can be traced, both proactively and reactively, to the prevailing Brahminical ethic that dominated the early, pre-*Gītā,* scene. This was the ethic of the sacrificial fire-rite, the *yajña* which bridged the world of the "gods" *(devas)* who dwelt immortal in heaven, and of humans steeped in their familiar web of earthly limitations. Proper performance of the *yajña* would give its human beneficiaries greater mastery over the unpredictable frailties of this life (through the production of desired offspring, wealth and wellbeing; victory in battle, and so on), and a share in the deathless company of the gods in the next. But this was a transactional ethic of action: the gods thrived on the sacrifice, while in turn the humans, through the good offices of their heavenly benefactors, enjoyed the desired "fruits" *(phala)* of their sacrificial acts. Nevertheless even here, as Flood points out, human desire must be subordinated to *the purpose of the sacrifice* (*kratvartha)*: thus a process of the *cleansing of inordinate desire* had begun. It is one of the insights of Flood's essay that in traditional Brahminical ethics, all morally acceptable actions, in whichever sphere of the received fourfold classification they might be perceived to fall (*artha, kāma, dharma,* or *mokṣa),* must be legitimated by a desire to conform to their particular end: in short, must be cleansed of inordinate desire. Still, for many, the highest ideal of *mokṣa* or liberation (an ideal in place by the time of the *Gītā)* seemed to require a turning away from the desires of everyday living and its "lesser" ideals (*artha* or the acquisition of worldly substance, *kāma* or the pursuit of satisfaction, and *dharma* or the following of one's caste-duties and observances).

But the *Gītā* also confronts us with the other side of the ethic of desire, viz. an ethic not of withdrawal from the world *(nivṛtti)*, but of active engagement with it *(pravṛtti)*, through the offering up of one's everyday duties *(sva-dharma)* in devotion to the Lord (Krishna, the embodiment of deity: *avatāra)*. Though the *Gītā* has been subjected in the course of history to various religious interpretations, it is difficult to avoid the conclusion, both analytically and contextually, that it is an inherently theistic text (Lash, Brockington, Hirst, Killingley, Gupta, Johnson). Is not love desire itself — the very seed of desire — the desire to be at-oned with the Beloved in everything that one does? As Killingley notes, referring to the *Gītā*, Krishna or "God himself is desire, such as does not conflict with *dharma* (7.11)" (p. 70) — again, a reference to ordinate rather than to inordinate desire. In teaching surrender then to the love of God (*bhakti*: the genitive here must be understood as both a subjective and an objective genitive) in everything we do, surely the *Gītā* recommends the purification rather than the suppression of desire?

As if to acknowledge this tension at its heart, in a famous verse, innovatively yet profoundly, the *Gītā* seems to offer a solution:

> "You are qualified simply with regard to action, never with regard to its results. You must be neither motivated by the results of action nor attached to inaction" 2.47.[5]

Here is prescribed a course for action *in* the world, but not *of* the world. In the context of the love of God, this requires the abandoning of one form of desire (inordinate desire) and the espousing of another (ordinate). We commented earlier that the *Gītā* is an ambivalent text in its teaching about desire. But this ambivalence itself is not straightforward. Professor Lash expresses it succinctly:

> "When, therefore, I speak of the ambivalence of the treatment of desire in some of the Upaniṣads and in the *Gītā*, I am not referring to the fact that, in these texts, love works for good and ill, for both the wounding and the healing of the world. The ambivalence that I have in mind concerns the outcome rather than the process,

attends the question as to whether peace fulfils desire or springs from its suppression" (p. 5).

There lies the rub: it is not enough for knowers *(jñānīs)* of their *sva-dharma* to abstain from desiring the fruits of their actions (*karman)*, by offering them in devotion (*bhakti)* to God. The story does not end there. Ambivalence attends not only the doing of dharmic deeds, but their outcome. *Dharma* like desire, as a function of the human condition, is pervaded by ambivalence, as the epic of which the *Gītā* is a part teaches again and again, not least by the pyrrhic victory of the great battle at its heart. Like all great works, the *Gītā* is an *elusive* text. At one level — the level of practical action — its teaching is simple: Act with purity of intention for the love of God alone. At the level of reflection, however — in the sphere of outcomes, expectations, consequences — it immerses us in a world of ambivalence. Thus to abandon the fruits of our actions is also to abandon those comforting expectations we so readily build into our virtuous deeds — expectations concerning *how* those actions, once surrendered, *must* or *will* bear fruit in the world. That's God's business, says the *Gītā,* not ours.

The elusiveness of the *Gītā* is expressed in different ways. John Brockington demonstrates how hard it is to pin this scripture down both textually and contextually. Though he himself ventures an opinion as to its date (ca. 1st-3rd century CE) and its setting (the *Gītā* is an interpolation in the epic[6]), he guides us through the still active debate on both these issues. *Devotionally* and indeed, theologically, for Hindus, as I have pointed out elsewhere,[7] the *Gītā* is integral to the *Mahābhārata* narrative. Theoretically, it has given rise to a host of interpretations from its early history to the present day. The *Gītā* is a living text, as Hirst's essay illustrates so well,[8] not only by considering the interpretations of well-known modern religious figures and thinkers, but by recording the replies to her questions of a number of Conference participants: "Where is Kurukshetra, the *dharma*-field, in our lives today?", "What is the lived reality of *dharma,* its scope and limitations?". If the *Gītā* cannot stimulate reflection on these questions for those who consider it seriously, it is not worth its salt. But as Dr Hirst's essay indicates, the text *does* enter into a conversation with those who address it. Once again, the fact that this dialogue produces a wide range of interpretations is only to be expected — dialogue is nothing if not context-specific — yet the thrust of these conversations is to recommend moral, selfless action in the world. The

Gītā generates a tension between the hermeneutics of *nivṛtti* (withdrawal) and *pravṛtti* (engagement).

This tension is expressed in another key dilemma of the *Gītā*: that between moral constraint and moral choice, perhaps more to the point, between determinism and freedom *(mokṣa)*. For in any ethical path, of course, there must always be moral constraint: *dharma*, as every contributor points out, has its parameters. "It is better to practise your own inherent duty [*sva-dharma*] deficiently" says 3.35 "than another's duty [*dharma*] well. It is better to die conforming to your own duty; the duty of others invites danger" (Johnson's translation). But does this verse hint at a larger confining horizon to our moral actions, at least in the world of the *Gītā*, than the mere constraint of particular moral parameters? In his essay on freedom in the *Gītā*, Johnson is particularly concerned with this question. Is the ethics of the *Gītā* deterministic? he asks — that is, does the *Gītā* teach, not so much that if you wish to be dharmic ("virtuous/dutiful") then you must follow a particular course of action or way of life (*sva-dharma*), but rather that, one way or another, *you are not in charge of your destiny*, that, below the deceptive surface, the true agent of action within you and through you is another: either the forces of nature, *prakṛti*,[9] or, to take another tack, the Lord himself?[10] Your task, then, would be to grasp this fact, and, more or less resignedly, to allow that agent full expression — or, as Johnson puts it: "Far from there being an almost infinite number of equally valid options, the *Gītā* demonstrates that, in the light of reality [viz. a realisation of the way things really are], choice is no longer possible in any meaningful sense — that is to say, there is only *one* valid response" (p. 93).

But of course, as Johnson goes on to suggest, behind the rhetoric of the *Gītā* it is ultimately (moral) choice that counts, viz. (i) *choosing* to know what's what, the way things really are, the way nature's forces are wont to act within one, the way the Lord's inner presence is expressible in one's actions — in short, choosing to be a "knower" *(jñānī)* in this respect; (ii) *choosing* to act upon this knowledge in the appropriate way, by withdrawing from the fruits, but engaging in the action — in short, choosing to be an agent (*kartā*) in this sense; and finally, (iii) *choosing* to act this way out of the love of God alone (*bhakti*) — that is, choosing to be a selfless devotee (*bhakta*). There is thus free choice all the way. This then is how I choose to interpret Johnson's own pregnant conclusion: "It is those two together — knowledge of the way things really are and acting in accordance with that knowledge — which are the ultimate liberating factors in the *Gītā*" (p. 94).

Indeed, Johnson has pointed to a *dialectical* teaching of the *Gītā,* the dialectic, that is, between choice and necessity, between freedom and determinism. We are free to choose, but not as free as we might believe: deeper forces within us continue to have their say in the outworking of our acts, mental and physical; again, there are powerful constraints to moral action, not only moral (and physical) constraints but also deep psychological ones, yet a core of moral autonomy remains intact. So it is that Krishna can say, after instructing Arjuna at length: "Such is the knowledge I have imparted to you, the mystery of mysteries; consider it fully, then do what you will" (18.63; Johnson's translation).

From the *Gītā*'s point of view, we are now in a position to respond to Ashis Gupta's pertinent questions: "Do we turn away from the fruits of our desiring? Do we let the fruits wither away on their branches?" In his striking essay, Gupta is primarily concerned to inquire into the relationship between *artha* or wealth and the *Bhagavadgītā.*[11] With great insight and in highly relevant ways in the context of economic constraints of today, he sketches a *Gītā*-based scenario of economic action for our times. But this concern merely focuses the larger issues raised by his two questions. According to the *Gītā,* we do not turn away from the fruits of our desiring, we may respond, rather, we transmute them through the *ultimate* fruit of our desiring — the selfless love of God — and in this light are free to pluck them and to enjoy them, for in thus enjoying them we acknowledge and enjoy the gracious boon-bestowing (*varada*) presence of God within us. In this, I venture to say, the *Gītā*'s project of discipleship is similar to the Christian's as described by Professor Lash, a project "conceived as lifelong schooling in the *purification* of desire, [as] a matter of discovering that, whatever we desire, our desiring of it is only the desire of God in the measure that it is conformed to and transformed by God's previous desire of us. Our yearning, purified, shares in that yearning by which the world is made"[12] — or, as the *Gītā* would say, by *lokasaṃgraha,* "maintaining the world" (3.20,25; Johnson). To do this, we must steer clear, the *Gītā* teaches, "of [inordinate] desire, anger, and greed — the threefold gates of hell" (Gupta, p. 81). In short, thus purified, we do not let the fruits "wither away on their branches". The "visionaries" (Gupta), the true "knowers" *(jñānī)* of *artha, kāma, dharma,* and *mokṣa* can pursue each or all of these goals with equal freedom for the very reason that in their true light, as explained above, they are not mutually divergent — as perhaps they would be in terms of the transactional ethic of sacrificial action discussed earlier — but are, rather, *of a piece with one other,* convergent goals subsumed under a common End, which is the ultimate fruit of our desiring. This, I believe, is the true teaching of the *Gītā* for our times, as endorsed by this important collection of essays. I have but outlined the bones of the argument; it is for the reader to clothe it with the enriching texture of what follows.

1 The subsequent Conferences of the Institute to date, viz. "A Body of Knowledge? The Relationship between Yoga and Science" (December 1st-2nd, 1995), and "Youth and Youthfulness in the Hindu Traditions" (July 5th-6th, 1996), were equally well appreciated, and it is hoped that their proceedings will also be published in a suitable form. I am grateful to Mrs Tessa Rodgers for her careful proof-reading of this book.

2 Cf. Johnson: "So rather than all action being, at some level, soteriologically significant, the *Gītā* teaches virtually the opposite: that all action — action in itself — is soteriologically *insignificant,* with the proviso, of course, that the underlying attitude of non-attachment prevails in all cases" (p. 101).

3 Killingley notes: "Perhaps the most frequent occurrence of desire in the *Bhagavadgītā* is in the form of something to avoid. For this reason, many of the terms for desire...occur with a negative prefix *niḥ-* or *a-* ". (p. 70). This does not mean, of course, that this is the main emphasis or teaching of the *Gītā* on desire.

4 *Mutatis mutandis,* a similar preference for contemplation over action might be endorsed within religio-cultural contexts other than the Hindu.

5 From W J Johnson's Penguin Translation, 1994.

6 "One cannot, it seems to me, sensibly regard the *Bhagavadgītā* as both integral to the epic and theologically profound"; (p. 30).

7 See *Hindus: their religious beliefs and practices,* 1994: 135

8 Cf. Killingley: "The variety of interpretations is evidence of its vitality" (p. 75).

9 See e.g. *Gītā* 3.5: "For no one ever, even for a moment, exists without acting; everyone, regardless of their will, is made to peform actions by the constituents [*guṇas*] which originate from material nature [*prakṛti*]", and 3.27: "In every case, actions are performed by the constituents of material nature [*prakṛti*]; although the man who is deluded by egotism thinks to himself, "*I* am the actor" (Johnson's translations). Today, people may refer to one's "genetic make-up" in this deterministic way.

10 "Arjuna, in the centre of the heart of all beings their lord stands still, mechanically revolving all creatures through his magical power", 18.61 (Johnson's translation).

11 See note 1 of Gupta's essay for the aptness of translating *artha* by "wealth" in this context.

12 p.6; emphasis added.

1

The Purification of Desire

NICHOLAS LASH

SOUNDING SILENCE

During the course of a seminar on Vivekananda, organised by the Indian Council of Philosophical Research, which took place in Hyderabad in March 1994, Professor Satchidananda Murty recalled a conversation he had had, many years before, with the great German philosopher, Karl Jaspers. Jaspers told Murty that he thought the *Bhagavadgītā* to be full of contradictions. Then, after a pause, he added: "That is why it is a great book".[1]

Jasper's compliment, itself not entirely lacking in ambiguity, reinforced my recognition of the difficulty of the task facing me. As the programme for the Conference says: the teachings of the *Gītā* "have been studied, commented upon and followed by countless human beings down the ages, and continue to exercise a profound influence not only in India but around the world". What on earth could induce an amateur (and I am the only speaker at our Conference who is not an expert student of the *Gītā*) to risk some comments on a text so burdened by interpretative wisdom? The answer, of course, is: Julius Lipner's remarkable powers of persuasion.

When, as a Christian theologian, I read the *Gītā*, I recognise, in its treatment of desire, an ambivalence that I have met elsewhere: an ambivalence as to whether the peace at which our hearts are set *fulfils desire or springs from its suppression.* It is this ambivalence on which I propose to offer one or two reflections.

In the Introduction to his edition of the *Gītā,* Antonio de Nicholas, taking a theme from St John of the Cross, spoke of that "'sounding silence' in which the world of the *Gītā* is submerged, and which we must recover if we are to give the *Gītā* its own meaning".[2] Consider, then, to set the scene, two images of "sounding silence". First, that strange announcement, at the *Gītā's* ending, that this whole conversation between Krishna and Arjuna — overheard by Saṃjaya through the din of impending battle: the thunder of drums, the conch shells' trumpeting, the shouts of men and cries of animals — is hidden, a secret.[3] What, we might ask, are the conditions for hearing silence that thus sounds?

For my second image, I turn to the first *Book of Kings* in the Hebrew Bible. The prophet Elijah, exhausted by failure and the overthrow of all he holds most dear, his own life under threat, withdraws to the wilderness. The silence of that place is interrupted by earthquake, wind and fire — the standard panoply, we might say, of God's appearance — but (the text insists) the Lord was not in any of them. "And after the fire a still small voice. And when Elijah heard it, he wrapped his face in his mantle and went out and stood at the entrance of the cave", to await God's fresh instructions.[4]

The moral I would draw from these two images is that God does not shout. Sometimes, as in the garden of Gethsemane, the stillness of God's speaking may be well-nigh unbearable. But, however we would wish it, God does not shout and, if we shout, we shall neither hear each other nor the holy mystery which calls us and commands the way we are to go.

Memory, Desire and Hope

The *Chāndogya Upaniṣad* speaks of "the real city of Brahman", wherein "all desires are contained", as the place where we are "free from sin, free from old age, free from death, free from sorrow, free from hunger, free from thirst" (8.1.5).[5] This city is, it seems, quite evidently not where we are *now.* It lies *beyond* our present circumstance. But where might that place be? Different cultures differently envisage the relationships between the here and now, and where things, by God's grace, are ultimately seen to be. If you will forgive the dangerously large-scale generalisation, I suggest that, at least where shaping frameworks of imagination are concerned, Upanishadic wisdom has its heart set deeper down, beyond the surface of the world, whereas the Christian heart is set beyond this time, beyond the edge of time, towards the dawning of eternity. As a slogan for this observation, we might say that Hindu metaphysics is correlative to Christian metachronics.[6]

And thus it is, for instance, that, within the more temporally structured Christian scheme of things, the ineradicability of the fact and memory of suffering generates a sense of tragedy which (I gather from the commentators) is not similarly found in Sanskrit literature.

Both Christianity and Hinduism, for example, give a central place to myth or epic, to that "once upon a time" whose purport rests precisely on the fact that no time in particular is thereby mentioned! But there is not, I think, in Indian sacred literature, a sentence bearing the weight borne, in Christianity, by "suffered under Pontius Pilate".[7]

The point I want to emphasise, however, is that the character of remembrance shapes the character of expectation and desire. Differences of memory engender differences of hope. These differences are, of course, not absolute. In Hinduism, as in Christianity, peace and harmony are held out as all things' hoped-for goal and destiny. And, in some texts, that *mokṣa* in which our peace and freedom from the travails of this world consists is characterised in terms that come quite close to Christian accounts of "beatific vision", of knowing even as we are known.[8]

It is, moreover, for Christian and Hindu alike, the groundedness of truth in gift which renders the purification of our understanding from the illusory forms with which egotism invests it, so peremptory and permanent a task. But: is such purification to be understood as *the cleansing of desire,* or *as its abolition?* That is the issue on which I wish to concentrate, and the construal of passages that speak of peace and harmony as the promised end of human longing is made more difficult by an ambivalence which, especially in the English translations (a point to which I will return), attends the treatment of desire.

"Desire", says the creation hymn in the *Ṛg Veda,* "came upon that one in the beginning; that was the first seed of mind".[9] According to R Panikkar (who translates *kāma,* in that passage, as "love" rather than "desire"), "Primordial love is neither a transitive nor an intransitive act.....it is the constitutive act by which existence came into being. Without love there is no being".[10] And de Nicholas says that "Desire is the fountain of creation in Indian philosophy from the Ṛg Veda through the Upaniṣads to the Gītā".[11] Against this, however, we have to set such passages as these: "When all desires that cling to the heart are surrendered, then a mortal becomes immortal.....When all the ties that bind the heart are loosened, then a mortal becomes immortal"..... "The wise who, free from desires, adore the Spirit pass beyond the seed of life in death. A man whose mind wanders among desires, and is longing for objects of desire, goes again to life and death according to his desires. But he who possesses the End of all longing, and whose self has found fulfilment, even in this life his desires will fade away".[12]

And if, when we come to the *Gītā,* some passages seem to offer an interpretative thread, by distinguishing appropriate from inappropriate desire, others afford no such easy escape route from the dilemma. Thus, on the one hand, we have Krishna's announcement, "I am desire when this is pure, when this desire is not against *dharma*". Elsewhere, however, having told Arjuna that, "All is clouded by desire: as fire by smoke, as a mirror by dust", and that "Wisdom is clouded by desire, the everpresent enemy of the wise," Krishna commands him, "Be a warrior and kill desire, the powerful enemy of the soul"[13]

These last three phrases, from the closing verses of chapter three, seem, in Mascaro's translation (which I am quoting) straightforwardly to identify the enemy as "desire". Winthrop Sargeant's version, however, clearly indicates that it is *rajas,* "passion arising from thirst and attachment", that is the enemy and not *kāma,* or desire, *as such,* although (and here I have 3.39 and 3.43 in mind) desiring will often be the form which egotism's restless passion takes.[14] In spite of which, Christopher Chapple, in his Introduction to the recently issued lavish new edition of Sargeant's translation, concludes his paraphrase of chapter three: "Only by subduing the senses and controlling the mind can desire be *overcome*".[15]

That "love" is both the fountain of creation and the enemy of the soul, that all things are created by desire and, by desire, destroyed — these fundamental facts about the world have been familiar, from the beginning, to all the great traditions. And thus it is that to be a Christian, or a Hindu, a Muslim or a Buddhist, is to know oneself apprenticed to a school the purpose of whose pedagogy is *the purification of desire.*

Moreover, notwithstanding the diversity of language and belief, of devotion and philosophy, of spirituality and social ethics, not only among all these traditions but within each one of them, it would be generally agreed that egotism lies at the root of love's destructive power. "Can that be Love", asked the poet William Blake, "that drinks another as a sponge drinks water?"[16] Egotism is the inability or refusal to relate, to find one's place, to make one's contribution to the whole. The unquiet self, driven either to dominance or self-destruction, knows no house, can find no resting-place, no peace. Egotism, in the last resort, is the denial, by the creature, of its createdness.

When, therefore, I speak of the ambivalence of the treatment of desire in some of the Upaniṣads and in the *Gītā,* I am not referring to the fact that, in these texts, love works for good and ill, for both the wounding and the healing of the world. The ambivalence that I have in mind concerns the outcome rather than the process, attends the question as to whether peace fulfils desire or springs from its suppression.

Consider the contrast between *Gītā* 2.70 and 2.71. "He attains peace into whom all desires flow like water entering the sea". According to Zaehner, this is an image of fulfilment, of desire "sublimated into tranquillity". "The man who abandons all desires, and acts without yearning, without possessiveness, without ego (not making himself to be the doer), he finds peace". This verse Zaehner sees as expressing the "Buddhistic ideal of the total severance of the temporal *(saṃsāra)* from the eternal *(nirvāṇa),* which in practice means the total *suppression* of desire".[17]

Does the contrast between these verses need to be drawn *quite* as sharply as Zaehner does, and in quite that manner? I once had the good fortune to visit Borobudur, in Java. To climb those great terraces, moving from the energetic complexity of the reliefs at the lower levels to the still simplicity of the stupas at the top, with an ever-broadening vista of the surrounding countryside as one does so, is to wonder whether at least the Buddhism that built *that* place, that seven-storied mountain, was not dedicated rather to the purification than to the "suppression" of desire.

The Desire of God

Let me come at the question from a different angle, by briefly reflecting on the theme of the desire of God. To speak of "the desire of God" is to speak ambiguously, because the phrase may mean either our desire of God or God's desire of us. Perhaps we might say that the Christian project of discipleship, conceived as lifelong schooling in the purification of desire, is a matter of discovering that, whatever we desire, our desiring of it is only the desire of God in the measure that it is conformed to and transformed by God's previous desire of us. Our yearning, purified, shares in that yearning by which the world is made.

Amongst the streams that have flowed into the broad river of Christian reflection on the love of God, and on the forms which human love will take in the measure that it is conformed to God's prior love of us, I will mention three: "Love as Greek *eros* was experienced and understood to be transformed by divine *agapé* into Augustine's *caritas*".[18] We can no longer translate *caritas* as "charity", because this has now degenerated into our preferred description for those devices by means of which connivance at injustice wears the mark of generosity. For Aquinas, however, *caritas* was a kind of *friendship,* and that's a better word, for, with its use, we are brought to the extraordinary discovery that human friendship — desiring purified into mutual, selfless, generous giving — may be the earthly form of the unknown, holy mystery of the world's creation, for God himself is met as friendship.[19]

You will notice that my detour through some of the Christian terminology has brought us back, at two levels, to the thought-world of the *Gītā.* First, at the ethical level, something very close to the purified desiring which Christians call *caritas* is proposed in 17.20: "The gift which is given only with the thought "it is to be given", to a worthy person who has done no prior favour, at the proper time and place, that gift is held to be *sattvic*" (that is Sargeant's translation).

There is, however, a second level of convergence, and it is theological. That, as our end and destiny, we are promised peace — the gathering into one circle of the scattered rays of light, the stillness of the ocean's depth, to use images of the *Praśna Upaniṣad*[20] — is, to put it mildly, far from obvious. But it is, perhaps, something we may learn and, in learning it, discover that we are desired by God. This quite extraordinary insight which, from Deuteronomy to the Fourth Gospel, is central to the message of the Jewish and the Christian scriptures, does not seem far from the lesson that Arjuna learns in hearing Krishna's secret word: "You are surely loved by Me", and, learning it, is enabled in tranquillity to respond, "I shall do as you command".[21]

I said, at the beginning, that I recognised in the *Gītā's* treatment of desire, an ambivalence as to whether the peace at which our hearts are set fulfils desire or springs from its suppression. By ambivalence, however, I do not quite mean "uncertainty", in the sense of undecidedness. The situation is more complex than that, and the grounds of its complexity lie not only in the text but also in the frameworks used for its interpretation.

The strength and richness of the tradition that finds expression in the *Gītā*, as of the tradition grounded in the New Testament that finds expression in the writings of Augustine and Aquinas, consists in no small measure in its refusal to rest content with, to settle for, partial or one-sided strategies and solutions, however plausible or attractive these may sometimes seem to be.

In other words, habits of thought and action dedicated to desire's suppression, rather than to the endless, strenuous labour, always to be freshly undertaken in each new set of circumstances, towards the purification of desire, are recognisable from within each of these traditions as distractions from, evasions of, the larger labour.[22]

A still, small Voice of Calm?

I once attended the funeral of a friend, the mother of two small children. It was a heart-rending occasion. Two of the hymns were selected by the children. Her four-year old daughter chose one of the best loved of all nineteenth-century hymns — "Dear Lord and Father of Mankind" — the last two verses of which go as follows:

> Drop thy still dews of quietness,
> Till all our strivings cease.
> Take from our souls the strain and stress,
> And let our ordered lives confess
> The beauty of thy peace.
> Breathe through the heats of our desire,
> Thy coolness and thy balm.

Let sense be dumb, let flesh retire,

Speak through the earthquake, wind, and fire,

O still, small voice of calm![23]

You will recognise in those last two lines Elijah's meeting with God in the wilderness, with which we began. But the sense has subtly shifted. Whereas Elijah heard, in that "sounding silence", God's command that (like Arjuna) he should return to action, the hymn, as one commentator puts it, "gains all its force from the presentation of the Gospel as a source of almost platonic repose, not as a judgement or a challenge".[24] The hymn, we might say, looks to the suppression of desire rather than to its purification.

But the story does not end there. The hymn comprises five of the last six verses of a poem written in 1872 by a New England Quaker named John Greenleaf Whittier. It will interest you to know that the title of the poem is "The Brewing of Soma", and that its text is prefaced by a verse from the *Sāma Veda,* in Max Müller's translation: "These libations mixed with milk have been prepared for Indra. Offer Soma to the drinker of Soma". The world is smaller than we sometimes think. Here are three verses from the earlier part of the poem.

"Drink, mortals, what the gods have sent,

Forget your long annoy".

So sang the priests. From tent to tent

The Soma's sacred madness went,

A storm of drunken joy.

The morning twilight of the race

Sends down these matin psalms.

And still with wondering eyes we trace

The simple prayers to Soma's grace,

That Vedic verse embalms.

And yet the past comes round again,

And new doth old fulfil.

In sensual transports wild as vain

We brew in many a Christian fane

The heathen Soma still![25]

The issue is narcotics. With that insouciance concerning the whereabouts of India and the identity of Indians that has characterised Western imperialism since Columbus' day, the New Englanders named as "Soma" a herb from which native Americans brewed an intoxicant which they used to engender ritual ecstasy. The poem contrasts such behaviour — this "drunken joy", these "sensual transports", "heats of our desire", deemed characteristic of benighted primitives (intimated by the phrase "The morning twilight of the race") — with the tranquillity of Christian experience, viz. an experience of "ordered lives", all strivings ceased, of "coolness" and of "balm". But, as we have seen, tranquillity has many faces. It may be the form of purified desire, maturity attentive to the sounding silence; but it may also, as suppression, be an evasion of responsibility, distraction from the labour to be undertaken in the name of friendship and in the service of our promised peace.

God does not shout. And yet the still, small voice Arjuna heard, against the noise of battle, was a stimulus to action. The still, small voice Elijah heard enjoined him to renew the struggle for God's cause. The sounding silence in Gethsemane commanded Calvary's commitment, the pure desire of Jesus — as of Arjuna — that God's will be done.

1 Quoted from F Wilfred, 1995: 338-9.
2 A de Nicholas, 1990: 5.
3 18.75
4 1 Kings, 19.12. Revised Standard Version.
5 S Radhakrishnan, 1953: 689.
6 See C Butler, 1967: 148-9.
7 See Lipner's discussion of the translation of itihāsa by "epic" (1994: 125). It is not without significance that when, in his discussion of "remembering", Lipner says that "smṛti recalls exemplary figures and events of 'the past'" (p.75), the last two words should be in inverted commas. On this whole question, Halbfass' cautious judgement is that, "The non-historical mode of self-presentation is still significant in modern Hindu thought and self-awareness" (1988: 367).
8 See I Corinthians, 13.12.
9 Ṛg Veda, 10.129.4, quoted from W D O'Flaherty, 1981: 25.
10 R Panikkar, 1977: 57; cf.p.58.
11 op.cit., p.145. It is, admittedly, not kāma that he is glossing here but the yathā icchasi tathā kuru of Gītā 18.63.
12 Kaṭha Upaniṣad, 2.3.14,15, Muṇḍaka Upaniṣad, 3.2.1,2. Where no indication of edition is given, I am using J Mascaro, 1965.
13 J Mascaro, 1962: 7.11, 3.38, 39, 43.
14 C Chapple, 1994: 14.7; 3.39.
15 C Chapple, 1994: xv (my stress).
16 William Blake, "Visions of the Daughters of Albion" (7.17). See G Keynes, 1972: 194. I am grateful to Michael Kirwan, S.J., for drawing my attention to this line.
17 Gītā, 2.70, 71 (de Nicholas). R C Zaehner, 1969: 157-8. For the penultimate phrase, Zaehner has "who does not think, 'This I am', or 'This is mine'".
18 D Tracy, 1994/6: 39.
19 See Thomas Aquinas, Summa Theologiae, IIa IIae, qq.23-30.
20 4,2; 6,5.
21 Gītā 18.64, 73 (Sargeant).
22 I would add that English-speaking readers of the Gītā are not helped by the tendency for translators, insufficiently familiar with the comparable richness and complexity of Western moral philosophy and Christian theology, to construe the concept of "desire" within far too narrow a range of sense and connotation.
23 J G Whittier, 1895: 462.
24 E Routley, 1952: 231. I am grateful to my colleague, Dr David Thompson, for drawing my attention to this and some other material concerning Whittier's poem.
25 Whittier, op.cit., p.461.

The Meaning and Context of the Puruṣārthas

GAVIN FLOOD

The *puruṣārthas*, the human purposes or goals of "virtuous behaviour" or "moral responsibility" *(dharma)*, "worldly success" *(artha)*, "pleasure", "desire" or "love" *(kāma)*, and "salvation" in the sense of "spiritual liberation" *(mokṣa)*, have had an important place in the history of Indian thought. They are important firstly because they codify central concerns of Hinduism, and secondly because they are categories developed within Hindu theology's self-understanding. They are part of a meta-discourse or the reflection of the tradition upon itself. In this essay I will first outline the history and meaning of the system of the *puruṣārthas*; secondly, I will develop a more thematic approach, examining the *puruṣārthas* as a discourse about a Hindu anthropology and theology which are concerned with the location of values and their expression in practice. Lastly, I shall comment on the relevance of the *puruṣārthas* in the contemporary world.

While at first appearing to be a straightforward list of human concerns — moral duty and obligation, wealth and success, pleasure, desire and love, and spiritual liberation — the list of the *puruṣārthas* nevertheless contains within it a number of philosophical and sociological issues or tensions concerning the nature of the self, the relation of means to ends, world rejection in contrast to world affirmation, the possibility of human agency in contrast to a heteronomy, and, particularly important in the contemporary world, gender issues and the degree to which the *puruṣārthas* are to be read as gender-specific. Some of these tensions can be seen in the history of the list and the order of importance attributed to each member. While the terms *dharma* and *mokṣa* occur from quite an early period in Indian literature, their coming together in the list of the *puruṣārthas* is a much later occurrence. It might be argued that the *puruṣārthas* as a structure represent a synthesis of two distinct value systems. The one, expressed in the figure of the householder, concerned with social obligation, with a high regard for the world-affirming values of wealth, success and sexual love; the other, expressed in the figure of the renouncer, concerned with the world-transcending value of liberation from suffering and rebirth through the renunciation of the householder's life, expressed as detachment, poverty and celibacy.

The Meaning and History of the Puruṣārthas

I should like to develop two related ideas. The first is that the *puruṣārthas* are a way of structuring the concept of the self (and body) in Hindu discourse at philosophical and sociological levels, expressed in formal treatises, as well as in poetry and legend. The second, is that the *puruṣārthas* can be regarded at a sociological level as "fields" or "provinces of meaning" with varying degrees of autonomy, which structure human agency. But first let us examine the meaning of the term and the understandings of the human subject it entails in Hindu texts.

(i) *The Meaning of the term*

The term *puruṣārtha* can be generally translated as a purpose or goal of man, or in less androcentric language, the purpose of human life or even the meaning of human life. The term itself is a masculine noun comprising two words, *puruṣa* or "man", and *artha* or "purpose" which together form a sixth-case *tatpuruṣa* compound; that is, the relation of the second term *artha* to the first term *puruṣa* can be taken to be a genitive relation, viz. "a purpose or purposes of humans". The term *artha* occurs here in the sense of goal or purpose and reappears again within the list where it indicates worldly success, particularly political success, and profit. The term *artha* can also mean "object", with the implication that such an object is known or perceived in a particular way, through a particular means of knowledge. The semantic fields of each of the terms in the system of the *puruṣārthas* are difficult to capture in a single

English word, and for a full account — beyond the scope of the present essay — each term would itself require a careful analysis of its textual occurrences and the contexts in which it is used. But one of the clearest statements offering some definition of the *puruṣārthas* is in the second chapter of Vātsyāyana's *Kāma Sūtra*. Here he defines *dharma* as adherence to sacred scripture, *artha* as wealth and its acquisition, and *kāma* as the proclivity *(pravṛtti)* towards pleasure, notably sexual pleasure, gained through the senses, especially touch.[1] *Kāma* can thus be rendered as both "desire", above all "sexual desire", as well as the object of that desire, namely "pleasure", though the connotation of *kāma* is wider than either "desire" or "pleasure", and incorporates "love" and its varying objects within its semantic field (including aesthetic objects).

(ii) *The Occurrences of the term in Brahminical discourse*

To understand the system of the *puruṣārthas*, we must locate the expression itself and the terms of its components in the context of the Brahminical discourse in which they occur. The *puruṣārthas*, or the equivalent expressions, the "group of three" *(trivarga)*, and "group of four" *(caturvarga)*, are found in mainstream Brahminical texts which look to the Veda as "revelation", but the expressions do not seem to occur in the Śaiva sources I am familiar with, underlining the system as central to orthopraxic, and arguably predominantly, Vaiṣṇava concerns.

One of the earliest occurrences of the term *puruṣārtha* is with the Pūrva Mīmāṃsā contrast between *puruṣārtha*, a human purpose, and *kratvartha*, a sacrificial purpose. This distinction is used in the context of determining the way in which the grades of authority of Vedic injunctions *(vidhi)* can be discerned. *Puruṣārtha* here refers to sacrificial acts done for the welfare and happiness of the sacrificer, *kratvartha* to sacrificial acts done for the sake of the sacrifice itself, beyond any particular human consideration. A Glucklich has shown that violation of *kratvartha* injunctions causes a defect in the sacrifice, rendering it inefficacious, whereas a violation of the *puruṣārtha* injunction causes the performer pollution while not affecting the sacrifice itself.[2] The *puruṣārtha* is the way in which the sacrificial patron makes the rite intelligible, the way he relates it to the world of human meanings, hopes and desires. Jaimini (ca.200 BCE) says in the *Mīmāṃsā Sūtra*, "What is pleasing for a man is not separable from the goal he wishes to obtain".[3] On this account, the result *(phala)* of the sacrifice is the consequence of the purpose *(artha)* of performing it. It is desire for results — particularly heaven upon death — which relates humans to the sacrifice and makes the sacrifice relevant to human interests.[4] *Kratvartha* by contrast is concerned with the internal coherence and structure of the sacrifice according to Vedic injunctions: making sure that the correct material is used at the correct time and so on, thereby placing the structure of ritual above human intentions.

Having undertaken a sacrifice as a consequence of a desire, the sacrificer soon learns that his *puruṣārtha* is just one perspective in the whole context of the sacrifice and that his intentions and desires must, as Francis Clooney has shown, be subordinated to the sacrificial purpose *(kratvartha)*.[5] Here human purposes are subordinated to the structure of the ritual; the human is "de-centred" to use Clooney's term, and subordinated to timeless Vedic injunction and to the objective action which that enjoins. To quote Jaimini, "The man is for the purpose of the action".[6] While recognising the power and reality of human purpose and desire, the Mīmāṃsakas subordinate it to a level below the objective structure and requirements of the ritual. The Veda and its injunctions are impersonal *(apauruṣeya)*.

For the Mīmāṃsakas then, we see that *puruṣārtha* and *kratvartha* are purposes or intentionalities which fulfil *dharma,* where *dharma* is understood as the cosmic order expressed in the laws of the sacrifice (the series of injunctions *(vidhi)* about ritual action *(karma)*. In a problematic passage Jaimini defines *dharma* as "the meaning expressed by Vedic utterance".[7] Vedic utterance, *codana,* specifically refers here to the power which authorises Vedic injunctions *(vidhi),* which in turn produces action, which in turn results in a transcendent power called *apūrva,* which results in the reward in heaven for the ritual patron. Heaven rather than *mokṣa* is the result of ritual action, yet even this *puruṣārtha* is ultimately subordinated to the real reason for performing the sacrifice, namely the Vedic injunction. The human goal *(puruṣārtha)* of heaven is almost an epiphenomenon of the sacrifice.

With the Śāstraic literature, in contrast to the Mīmāṃsakas, an anthropology is presented with far greater emphasis on human desires and aspirations. In this literature, which had probably reached its present form by 2nd century CE, though its origins are earlier, the *puruṣārthas* as a system of three goals is articulated. The term *puruṣārtha* in the Smṛti texts came to refer to human purposes rather than to an element in the fulfilling of an impersonal cosmic order. While these purposes are brought together as a system in these texts, each of the constituent terms of the *puruṣārthas* occurs outside of that context and has its own history. Of particular note are *dharma* and *mokṣa. Dharma* is the older term, occurring as early as the *Ṛg Veda,*[8] though as Halbfass notes, there is surprisingly no systematic monograph on an analysis and history of the term's usage.[9] The noun *mokṣa,* derived from the root *muc,* occurs in the later Upaniṣads,[10] though the verbal form *mucy-* is found in the earliest Upaniṣads, the *Bṛhadāraṇyaka* and the *Chāndogya.*[11] The term *apavarga,* a synonym for *mokṣa* — that which is opposite the group of three purposes *(trivarga)* — occurs only relatively late in the *Maitrī Upaniṣad.*[12]

The *puruṣārthas* would at first appear to be the object of different groups of texts: the Dharma Śāstra focusing on *dharma,* the Artha Śāstra on *artha,* and the Kāma Śāstra on *kāma.* However, the *puruṣārtha* system is not a typology of Śāstras, but functions within those texts as an expression of those texts' varying objects. While the treatises on *dharma* would no doubt acknowledge their primary object of attention to be *dharma,* it is only Kauṭilya's *Arthaśāstra* and Vātsyāyana's *Kāma Sūtra* (modelled on the former), which locate themselves consciously within the *puruṣārtha* scheme. There are other texts, principally in Sanskrit but also in Tamil, in which references to the *puruṣārthas* are found, most notably in the epics, narrative traditions such as the Pañcatantra, and in drama and poetry (such as Bhartṛhari's *Śatakatraya).* They are also mentioned in the Purāṇas, and are assumed in philosophical literature.

In the Śāstraic literature, the system of the *puruṣārthas* refers to the "group of three" *(trivarga)* — *dharma, artha,* and *kāma* — rather than a "group of four" *(caturvarga)* which includes *mokṣa.* The *Arthaśāstra* refers to three aims,[13] as do the *Manu Smṛti,*[14] and the *Bhagavadgītā,*[15] where these are the legitimate pursuits of a man in the second or householder's stage *(āśrama)* of life, though these texts also discuss *mokṣa* outside the context of this system. In the Śāstras *dharma* is regarded as a human purpose, a human intention, though a higher human intention than profit or pleasure. "The knowledge of *dharma",* Manu says, "is enjoined for those who are unattached to profit and pleasure".[16] Indeed, the hierarchy of the terms is reinforced by Manu's relating the goals to the three *guṇas* or qualities which pervade existence, of lightness *(sattva),* passion *(rajas),* and darkness or inertia *(tamas).*[17]

The term *dharma* here has come to have a wider connotation than the more technical Mīmāṃsaka conception of correct sacrificial procedure, as the highest human intention that it is possible to have. With the Śāstras, and indeed with epic literature, *dharma* has come to have great personal and social relevance beyond ritual considerations. As Halbfass says, "In traditional and "orthodox" Hinduism, *dharma* appears as an essentially anthropocentric, sociocentric, and, moreover, Indocentric and Brahmanocentric concept".[18] Beyond ritual injunction *dharma* has come to mean the socio-cosmic order and particularly the order expressed in the *varṇāśrama-dharma* formula. Yaśodhara in his commentary on the *Kāma Sūtra* (2.7), the *Jayamaṅgala,* says that *dharma* means inclination towards certain actions, particularly the accomplishment of ritual, and detachment from other actions which lead away from it. Manu lists ten characteristics or kinds of psychological states and actions which comprise dharmic behaviour, namely, patience *(dhṛti),* forgiveness *(kṣama),* self-control *(dama),* not-stealing *(asteya),* purification *(śauca),* restraint of the senses *(indriyanigraha),* intelligence *(dhī),* knowledge *(vidyā),* and lack of anger *(akrodha).*[19] These rather personalised attributes of the Brahmin are reminiscent of the ideal renouncer. But *dharma* most importantly refers not only to personal behaviour and attitudes, but also to social structures — the *varṇa* system — and to the duty of the king, the *rāja dharma,* which, Manu says, is primarily the imposition of justice or punishment *(daṇḍa).* The king who doles out justice thrives within the three categories *(trivarga).*[20]

Undoubtedly, as one would expect, *dharma* is the most important purpose of human life in the Dharma Śāstras. The *Gautama Dharma Śāstra* says that one should attach the most importance to *dharma,* as does the *Yājñavalkya Smṛti.*[21] The other two aims of profit and pleasure are legitimate, but must always be constrained by *dharma.* The *Āpastamba Dharma Sūtra* says that a man should enjoy all pleasures that are not opposed to *dharma,* in this way, "he secures both worlds" *(lokāv abhijayati);*[22] that is, he is successful in the present life and attains heaven or the world of the ancestors at death.

When profit and pleasure are pursued alone, outside of *dharma,* they lead to social chaos. This same idea is expressed in the *Gītā* where Krishna identifies himself with the desire in all beings which is not opposed to *dharma.*[23] Even Vātsyāyana, the champion of *kāma*, recognises the relative value of each of the goals. Profit, he says, is more important than pleasure or desire, social success more important than success in love, and *dharma* more important than success and wealth,[24] though Bhīma in the *Mahābhārata* sees *kāma* as the basis of the other concerns.[25]

There is nevertheless a tension between these three pursuits, and different texts foreground one of them at some cost to the others. Kauṭilya's *Arthaśāstra* sees *artha* as the basis or root *(mūla)* of the other two, for both *dharma* and *kāma* depend on it for their realisation.[26] Yet in the same passage he also says that they are interdependent and one should not be exaggerated over the others. He writes:

> "One should enjoy pleasure without ceasing from virtuous behaviour and wealth. One may then not be without happiness. One should enjoy equally the group of three which are mutually connected. Indeed, if only one of them is pursued, this harms either virtuous behaviour, wealth or pleasure [viz. the one that is being pursued] as well as the other two".[27]

The text here emphasises the co-dependence of the human purposes. They are "mutually connected" *(anyonyānubaddham)*, a term which implies or emphasises that each of the *puruṣārthas* is inextricably bound to the others. Indeed they are so interconnected that to pursue one at the expense of the others is harmful to the others, which can be taken to mean is harmful to the structure as a whole and so is harmful to the social matrix of which they are expressions. The system of the *puruṣārthas* functions in this text to structure the idea of the self and to articulate the constraints upon the person in a particular socio-political context. In the *Arthaśāstra, artha* refers primarily to political power rather than to wealth and success, through an attitude of ruthless political clarity in which the ten qualities of *dharma* listed by Manu are completely ignored.

(iii) Precedence in the Puruṣārthas

Which of the *puruṣārthas* predominates, is variable to some extent. There are proximate and ultimate ends,[28] and different goals will be appropriate for different people and roles at different times. The *Kāma Sūtra* makes it clear that *artha* should be the primary goal of the king. The text also suggests that different purposes are appropriate for different times of life. Indeed, the text opens with the statement that during a man's life he must pursue three aims successively: *kāma* should predominate in adulthood as should *artha,* while *dharma* and *mokṣa* should be practised in old age.[29] While Vātsyāyana establishes a connection between the *puruṣārthas* and the human lifespan, this is not a general pattern. Some modern scholars have attempted to identify the three or four aims with the four stages of life, the *āśramas*, in ways which are certainly coherent,[30] but as P Olivelle has pointed out, there is no textual basis for this and the *puruṣārthas* are nowhere identified with the four *āśramas*.[31]

The debate about precedence also occurs towards the end of the *Mahābhārata,* after the end of the war and after Aśvatthāman, one of the three remaining Kauravas, has slaughtered many in the Pāṇḍava camp in revenge over his father, Droṇa's, death. The five Pāṇḍavas are having a discussion with the wise Vidura about which of the *puruṣārthas* is most important.[32] Vidura claims that *dharma* is the most important, for through *dharma* the sages entered the Absolute, on *dharma* the universe rests, and through *dharma* wealth is acquired. Arjuna disagrees, claiming that *dharma* and pleasure rest on profit *(artha).* Bhīma argues for *kāma* as the primary goal, for without it even the ancient sages would not have attained liberation. And Yudhiṣṭhira agrees with Vidura, arguing that *dharma* should be the first goal, even though he finds it difficult to understand, and abiding by its dictates often goes against his nature.[33]

Although Manu does emphasise *dharma,* there is nevertheless one passage in which the text advocates not the primacy of any one of the *trivarga,* but the totality of them all. Rather than a successive hierarchy, they should be viewed as an interrelated whole. The human subject is not to be dominated by any single purpose, but rather fulfil various and divergent aspects of his or her being: "*Dharma* and wealth are said to be the best, or pleasure and profit, or just *dharma* or just wealth alone. But the established view is that the threefold system is the best".[34]

The Social Contexts of the Puruṣārthas

The system of the *puruṣārthas* is a theologoumenon, that is, the end result of a "theological" process or theoretical formulation of what humans do and aspire to do. The list is a way of structuring the human subject in relation to the body, social world and transcendence, and expresses both a theological and an anthropological discourse. This does not mean, of course, that the *puruṣārthas* did not and do not have practical consequences, but simply that they are formulated as an entity at a theoretical level. Indeed, the apparently innocent list of the *puruṣārthas* does not necessarily express a common vision concerning the human subject, but hides, rather, a tension and divergent views concerning, on the one hand, the nature of the self as a social actor embedded within a social world, and, on the other, the self as a transcendent entity beyond the social world.

The *puruṣārthas* express an understanding of the human subject — of human nature — and the conflicts which that inevitably entails. While it is fair to understand them as being insights into human nature and as acknowledging distinct human drives, viz. the need to fulfil responsibilities to one's kin group, the need for wealth (the negative side of which is acquisitiveness), the need for sexual love and for pleasure, and the need for a soteriological understanding of life, they can also, less generally, be seen as articulating the aspirations of particular social groups or levels within ancient Indian society and as expressing different models of self-understanding. The system of the *puruṣārthas* must be seen in the context of a Brahminical discourse of which it is a part, along with the *varṇa* and the *āśrama* systems which, as Olivelle has shown, is also a theological construct.[35] The *puruṣārthas* articulate and codify elements in early and classical Indian culture, drawing together different and perhaps conflicting value systems from a variety of social contexts: most notably a context of Brahminical orthopraxy (which has predominantly defined the value of *dharma)*, a context of a ruling aristocracy (in which primarily operate the values of *artha* and *kāma)*, and the context of world renunciation (in which predominates the value of *mokṣa).*

While the terms *dharma, artha, kāma* and *mokṣa* are all found as general terms outside of the *caturvarga* system, their coming together here indicates a recognition of social diversity as well as a belief in social coherence. They are recognitions of the constraints operating within human nature — the instincts or drives towards safety, love, and shelter — yet they also recognise, long before Freud, that the formation of culture depends upon their control and regulated expression, an expression which, at the level of discourse, was controlled by the Brahmins. Thus, on the one hand, the system of the *puruṣārthas* articulates a structure which might be said to constrain human energy in that it determines the kinds of actions which are appropriate in different contexts and by different social groups, yet on the other, it is an expression of agency in recognising the ability of social actors to choose their legitimate pursuits. The system of the *puruṣārthas*, existing at an ideological level as it does, might itself be regarded as an articulation of social actors reflecting upon the structure of their own traditions and affecting that structure through formulating the *puruṣārtha* system.[36]

The Place of Mokṣa

Yet there would seem to be a tension between the goals exclusively concerned with personal fulfillment in the context of social responsibility and, at least in some traditions, the "impersonality" of spiritual liberation. This tension is probably irresolvable, though texts try to make these goals compatible by constructing a hierarchy of purposes in which either *mokṣa* or *dharma* is presented as the apex of human achievement. The *Sāṃkhya Kārikā* of Īśvarakṛṣṇa (4th-5th cent. CE), for example, says that *dharma* leads only to ascent to a higher world *(gamanam ūrdhvam),* while knowledge or correct cognition *(jñāna)* leads to liberation which is beyond all worlds and categories *(apavarga):*

> "By means of virtuous behaviour, one attains a higher abode; by lack of virtuous behaviour one goes to a lower abode. By means of correct cognition, one obtains liberation and by the opposite, bondage".[37]

In contrast, for Manu, the fulfilling of dharmic obligations is supreme. Indeed, if a Brahmin, desiring liberation, relinquishes his dharmic responsibilities by becoming a renouncer, of fulfilling his three debts, studying the Veda and sacrificing, he goes to lower rebirths.[38]

By the time of Śaṃkara's commentary on the *Brahmasūtra* (ca.8th cent. CE), *mokṣa* has been incorporated into the *trivarga* to form a "group of four" *(caturvarga).*[39] Here *mokṣa* surpasses the other purposes as the highest human value, though it is not recognised by the Mīmāṃsakas until the eighth century with Kumārila. With the addition of *mokṣa,* the *trivarga* is transformed into a system of three + one; it has become a set of four, the importance of which in Indian culture has been demonstrated by Malamoud[40] and Olivelle.[41] This transformation of the *trivarga* into the *caturvarga* and the supplanting of *dharma* and the other two purposes by *mokṣa,* suggests that a confluence of different value systems has occurred. Put simply, a Brahminical worldview in which the highest values are ritual and social responsibility, pleasure, wealth and worldly success, has incorporated a worldview in which liberation and the transcending of the social world takes precedence.

The fourth goal of life, *mokṣa,* called the "supreme human purpose" *(paramapuruṣārtha),* stands apart from the other three and in many ways is opposed to them, expressing a goal of world-transcending liberation, socially or institutionally expressed in renunciation. The contrast between the three purposes and the last is also a contrast between the Brahmin householder and the renouncer. The early Mīmāṃsakas do not discuss *mokṣa,* and the Dharma Śāstras do not regard it as part of the system of the *puruṣārthas*, though they recognise its legitimate pursuit after the fulfilling of social obligations. But for the Vedānta, *mokṣa* is unequivocally the highest goal: the world-transcending liberation beyond *dharma* and the social world, attained by world renouncers.

In contrast to the Pūrva Mīmāṃsakas, the Uttara Mīmāṃsakas or Vedāntins subordinate, as one would expect, the three human purposes concerned with action or behaviour to the knowledge which is *mokṣa.* Indeed, whereas the three goals of *dharma, artha* and *kāma,* imply agency — albeit predominantly the agency of the Brahmin male — *mokṣa* implies the negation of agency and the renunciation of action. *Mokṣa* is knowledge of the self which is not an action for the Advaita Vedānta thinkers, nor an injunction, even though revealed in scripture. This final goal must take precedence over all others. Śaṃkara even says in his commentary on the *Gītā* that *dharma* is an obstacle to liberation because it produces links or attachments.[42] The final and highest human purpose here is knowledge of the deeper self or the Absolute *(Brahman),* which nevertheless is not a kind of thing which can be known as an object of knowledge, but a truth which is revealed by the Veda.[43]

This addition of *mokṣa* to the list reflects, as Karl Potter has observed, an important shift in worldview from an orientation which regards *dharma* as social obligation to be the highest human goal, to a worldview which elevates liberation above this.[44] These are different anthropological models which are being integrated here: on the one hand, a construction of the self and body as expressing a socio-cosmic system, on the other a negative appraisal of the socialised self and body in favour of a vision of the self as transcendent being. This distinction maintains a truly creative tension throughout the history of Hinduism, as can be seen not only in the Dharma literature, but also in the epics and narratives of Hinduism *(itihāsa, purāṇa),* Kāvya literature, and in the narrative traditions of vernacular languages, though this "tension" should not be exaggerated, as Ingalls has observed,[45] for there is often a perceived continuity from *dharma* to *mokṣa.*

That we generally find the *puruṣārthas* as a group of three in the Śāstras indicates that *mokṣa* has developed outside the context of Brahminical social values. R Thapar, among others, has shown that within ancient India there were two dominant religious ideologies and, indeed, social groups: Brahminism and Śramaṇism.[46] By Brahminism, she refers to the tradition of the Brahmins, the tradition of Vedic orthopraxy which revered the Veda as revelation; by Śramaṇism, she refers to traditions of generally itinerant world renouncers, the Śramaṇas, who rejected the authority of the Veda and pursued a lifestyle of asceticism and meditation. Early Buddhism and Jainism were two of these Śramaṇa traditions.

This distinction between the Brahmins and the Śramaṇas is recognised in the edicts of the emperor Aśoka, and the grammarian Patafestyle of asceticism and meditation. Early Buddhism and Jainism were two of these Śramaṇa traditions.[47] Brahminism revered the Veda and performed sacrifices in response to Vedic injunction, Śramaṇism emphasised the authority of individual experience and rejected the violence involved in the sacrifice. Indeed, the Śramaṇas reinterpreted the idea of the Brahmin as one who is morally upright and whose passions are controlled.[48] It would seem to be clear that during the latter half of the first millenium BCE, Śramaṇa traditions developed — perhaps linked to the urbanisation of the Ganges plain[49] — which were antagonistic towards or reinterpreted the religion of the Brahmins. While the focus of Brahminism was the performance of ritual and social behaviour enjoined by the Veda, the focus of Śramaṇism was on asceticism and meditation in order to achieve a spiritual liberation, variously conceptualised in different Śramaṇa traditions, but generally regarded as a liberation from action *(karman)* and the cycle of rebirth. Although Brahminism reasserted itself over Śramaṇism, the idea of liberation from action and the methods of its attainment entered mainstream Vedic religion.

On this account *mokṣa* and the value system associated with it of world renunciation, freedom from action, asceticism and, in the Upaniṣads, the internalisation of the Vedic ritual, developed within a Śramaṇic worldview, whereas the values of *dharma, artha* and *kāma* developed within a Brahminical worldview. The *trivarga* is an expression of Vedic orthopraxy, whereas the *caturvarga* is an indication of the assimilation by Brahminism of the Śramaṇic ideology of *mokṣa.*

But perhaps this is to paint a rather crude picture. J Gonda long ago warned us about the problems involved in discerning the "aryan" from the "non-aryan" and implicitly, the Vedic from the non-Vedic,[50] and Olivelle has shown how the term *śramaṇa* is related to the term *āśrama* — a highly orthopraxic concept.[51] Indeed, eminent scholars such as Heesterman and Biardeau have argued that renunciation and its attendant ideas of asceticism and meditation leading to *mokṣa,* can be derived from the Vedic tradition itself, that there is no need to postulate an externally derived ideology. Heesterman has called this the "orthogenetic theory" of the origins of renunciation.[52] While this is not the place to go into the arguments for and against Heesterman's thesis, the point I would wish to make is that, regardless of origins (whether "Vedic" or "non-Vedic"), we have expressed in the four *puruṣārthas* at least two distinct value systems which were located in different social groups during the first millenium BCE, but which are becoming fused together during the last centuries of this millenium and the first centuries CE. The *trivarga* of *dharma, artha* and *kāma* represents a Brahminical ideology and the adding of *mokṣa* to form the *caturvarga* represents the incorporation of a non-Brahminical worldview, possibly associated with the Kṣatriya aristocracy and possibly with other non-Brahminical segments of early Indian society.

Means and Ends

To summarise the discussion so far. We have seen that the system of the *puruṣārthas* contains within it tensions and conflicts over the ways in which the human subject is understood. Indeed, the *puruṣārthas* might be seen as an attempt to synthesise different ways of conceptualising the human subject, in terms on the one hand, of social obligation and an orientation towards the expression and fulfillment of desire, and on the other, of an orientation away from the social world and away from the expression of desire towards a transcendent soteriology. In many ways the *Bhagavadgītā* might be seen as an attempt to bring together the opposing tendencies found in the *puruṣārthas*. But it is significant that the list does contain divergent ideals and models of human nature brought together in a coherent way. It seems to be saying that there are distinct provinces of meaning or realms within the human world which can be recognised as legitimate pursuits and ends in themselves.

The system of the *puruṣārthas* implicitly recognises the complexity of human aspirations and drives. That these aspirations and drives are necessarily varied, is reflected in the different interpretations of the terms of the *puruṣārthas* within Hindu traditions and in regarding them as either ends in themselves, which demand specific means for their realisation, or as means to other ends. There is a relation between human goals and the methods whereby they are obtained. The Nyāya thinker Udayana says that the idea of a human goal entails the idea of the means of its realisation and these means in turn should be subject to analytical scrutiny *(ānvīkṣikī)*.[53] For the Mīmāṃsakas, wealth and desire are instrumental in achieving the sacrifice enjoined in the Veda, which, as we have seen, is both an end in itself and the means to fulfil the human purpose of heaven upon death. The Advaitins, such as Sureśvara, maintain that *mokṣa* as supreme happiness is an end in itself and the only truly valid human pursuit, though a goal that is not the result of a process *(sādhya)* but is constantly attained *(siddha)* through its realisation. [54] The highest goal of *mokṣa* on this account is technically not attained by any means of knowledge *(pramāṇa)*, but is realised through its revelation in the Veda, though the Veda cannot, of course, *cause* Brahman to be realised.

The Contemporary Relevance of the Puruṣārthas

We have surveyed some of the texts and suggested some ways in which the *puruṣārthas* can be historically located, and have noted that the *puruṣārtha* system is a synthesis of different value systems coming from different social strata of ancient Indian culture. The *puruṣārthas* are a synthesis, and arguably a successful synthesis (though see Daya Krishna for a counter-argument in this respect[55]), a pulling together of diverse cultural strands at a theoretical or discursive level. What relevance then, if any, does this list hold for the contemporary world? Certainly the *puruṣārthas* are a rich resource within Hinduism that the tradition can draw upon for the construction of itself in the modern world, and draw upon in issues of conflict and reconciliation among diverse communities, particularly in India. Traditionally the *puruṣārthas* have contributed to a Brahminical ideology of the self, and to the structuring of ideas about human agency and gender. Pursuing the goal of *dharma* has meant different things to different social groups; yet the power entailed or assumed in the pursuit of *artha* and indeed, *kāma*, has been beyond the significant capabilities of many people and the pursuit of *mokṣa* restricted, in strictly orthopraxic circles, to the twice-born male renouncer. The system of *puruṣārthas* has traditionally implied clearly defined role models for various social groups and for men and women. The primary aim of a woman, according to the Dharma Śāstras, is the fulfilling of her *strī-dharma*, to be without independence *(svatantra)*, and to be subject to the male authority of fathers, husbands and sons. Apart from her *strī-dharma*, *kāma* was regarded as the province of women, though mainly instrumentally for men.[56]

Yet significantly, the idea of the *puruṣārthas* still has meaning in contemporary Indian culture: the language of the *puruṣārthas* is still used. For example, the Indian feminist journal *Manushi*, in discussing female *bhakta* poets, uses the language of the *puruṣārthas* in describing these poets. One passage says:

> "These women [*bhakta* poets] contributed to the building of a culture wherein women who devote themselves to a pursuit of some goal higher than self-interest, and who demonstrate an ability to stay steadfast to their chosen ideals, are not made objects of derision, but are given special respect, even homage".[57]

Here we have a use of *puruṣārtha* terminology and a recognition that that terminology can be used as cultural critique from a feminist perspective. I should, however, mention that the text goes on to criticise this idea of a selfless goal, but the point is that the *puruṣārtha* terminology is being used and engaged with in highly relevant contemporary debate.

Relevant to contemporary debates about gender issues and agency, it is important to recognise that while the *puruṣārthas* can certainly be seen as an articulation of Brahminical orthopraxy, they also contain within them a pluralism and a recognition of difference. We can arguably regard the *puruṣārtha* system sociologically as expressing distinct and coherent "fields" or "provinces of meaning", to use

Alfred Shutz's phrase, with varying degrees of autonomy. By "sociological" I mean that the *puruṣārtha* system contains an implicit theory of society — formulated at the level of Brahminical discourse — and while existing at an ideological level, nevertheless expresses a social or number of social worlds. While human agency has been structured in traditional Hindu communities so as to constrain lower caste groups and women, the *puruṣārthas* might well function as a liberating ideology which recognises a plurality of human purposes and pursuits. The *puruṣārthas* potentially allow for people to "do their own thing", and can be interpreted as a non-prescriptive, fluid system whose meaning varies according to situation. The *puruṣārthas* could be said to express, to use a fashionable phrase, "context-sensitivity".

The relevance of the *puruṣārthas* for the modern world, and particularly for modern India with its conflicting cultural forces moving towards globalisation on the one hand, and towards a fragmented nationalism on the other, lies in their recognition of pluralism and the tolerance which that recognition entails. The *puruṣārthas* can potentially act as cultural critique in their implicit recognition of a plurality of social behaviours, their recognition of the need for prosperity and power, their recognition of the need for love and aesthetic experience, and in their recognition of the aspiration — in some — for a "spiritual" liberation. The *puruṣārtha* system can be reinterpreted for contemporary contexts. As a quotation from the works of Gandhi cited in *Manushi,* says: "It is good to swim in the waters of tradition, but to drown in them is suicide".[58]

1 Vātsyāyana, *Kāma Sūtra*, 2.8-12.
2 A Glucklich, 1988: 91-2.
3 *Mīmāṃsā Sūtra*, 4.1.2: yasmin prītiḥ puruṣasya tasya lipsārthalakṣaṇāvibhaktatvāt.
4 *Mīmāṃsā Sūtra*, 6.1.4. See F X Clooney, 1990: 141-3.
5 F X Clooney, 1990: 146.
6 *Mīmāṃsā Sūtra*, 3.1.6: *puruṣaś ca karmārthatvāt.*
7 *Mīmāṃsā Sūtra*, 1.1.2: *codanālakṣaṇo'rtho dharmaḥ.*
8 E.g. *Ṛg Veda*, 10.16.3.
9 W Halbfass, 1988: 311-2.
10 *Śvetāśvatara Upaniṣad*, 6.16; *Maitrī Upaniṣad*, 6.30.
11 *Bṛhadāraṇyaka Upaniṣad*, 3.8.12 (see also *mu.8.12* 1.5.17); *Chāndogya Upaniṣad*, 6.16.2.
12 *Maitrī Upaniṣad*, 6.30.
13 Kauṭilya *Arthaśāstra*, 1.7.3.
14 7.27, 7.151-2.
15 18.34.
16 2.13: *arthakāmeṣv asaktānāṃ dharmajñānaṃ vidhīyate.*
17 12.38. Manu gives the hierarchy as follows: *kāma*, *artha*, and *dharma*, corresponding to *tamas*, *rajas*, and *sattva*, in ascending order of excellence.
18 W Halbfass, 1988: 319-20.
19 6.92.
20 Manu, 7.27.
21 *Gautama Dharma Śāstra*, 1.9.46-7; *Yājñavalkya Smṛti*, 1.115.
22 *Āpastamba Dharma Sūtra*, 2.20.22-23.
23 7.11: "I am that desire in all beings not opposed to *dharma*": *dharmāviruddho bhuteṣu kāmo'smi.*
24 *Kāma Sūtra*, 2.14.
25 Mbh. 12.167 ff. (reference from and discussed in R C Zaehner, 1966: 115).
26 *Arthaśāstra*, 1.7.7.
27 *Arthaśāstra*, 1.7.3: *dharmārthāvirodhena kāmaṃ seveta, na niḥsukhaḥ syāt. samaṃ vā trivargam anyonyānubaddham. eko hy atyāsevito dharmārthakāmānām ātmānam itarau ca pīḍayati.*
28 Kane, vol.2, 1974: 8.
29 *Kāma Sūtra*, 2.2-4.
30 E.g. A Sharma, 1982.
31 P Olivelle, 1993: 218.
32 Śāntiparvan, 12.167.
33 For a discussion of this, see R C Zaehner, 1962: 115-7.
34 Manu, 2.224: *dharmārthāv ucyate śreyaḥ kāmārthau dharma eva ca; artha eveha vā śreyas trivarga iti tu sthitiḥ.*
35 P Olivelle, 1993: 24-7.
36 On structuration theory implicit in these comments, see A Giddens, 1984, and 1993: 78-99, 131-2.
37 *Kārikā* 44: *dharmeṇa gamanam ūrdhvam, gamanam adhastād bhavaty adharmeṇa; jñanena cāpavargo, viparyayād iṣyota bandhaḥ.*
38 Manu, 6.35-7.
39 See Śaṃkara's *Brahmasūtrabhāṣya*, 3.4.1.
40 C Malamoud, 1988: 33-48.
41 P Olivelle, 1993: 217.
42 See his *Gītābhāṣya* on 4.21.
43 The supreme human goal is, says, Bādarāyaṇa, due to revelation: *puruṣārthaḥ sabdād iti bādarāyaṇa* (*Brahmasūtra*, 3.4.1).
44 K Potter, 1991: 14-15.
45 D Ingalls, 1958: 48.
46 R Thapar, 1993: 62-84.
47 R Thapar, 1993: 63.
48 K R Norman, 1985: 50-51; see also J Heesterman, 1985: 42-3.
49 R Gombrich, 1988: 58-9.
50 J Gonda, 1965: 206. See also Olivelle, 1993: 35-6.
51 P Olivelle, 1993: 11-17.
52 J Heesterman, 1985: 40.
53 W Halbfass, 1988: 27.
54 M Hiriyanna, 1952: 85-87.
55 Daya Krishna, 1991: 189-205.
56 See M Biardeau, 1989: 46-52.
57 *Manushi*, Tenth Anniversary Issue, p.6
58 Ibid.

3 The Bhagavadgītā: Text and Context

JOHN L BROCKINGTON

THE GĪTĀ AND THE MAHĀBHĀRATA

To most Vaiṣṇavas, and indeed to most modern Hindus, the *Bhagavadgītā* (Mbh.6.23-40) is their main religious text and the real source of many of their beliefs, even though as part of one of the epics it falls outside the canon of authority *(śruti),* and it is nearly as well known nowadays in the West. Its setting is the impending battle between the Kurus and the Pāṇḍavas, which forms the heart of the great epic, the *Mahābhārata,* and in form it consists of a long dialogue, which is virtually a monologue, between Arjuna and Krishna. It is, indeed, really more of a sermon which Krishna delivers to Arjuna as the two armies stand drawn up in battle array, waiting to commence the battle which is the climax of the *Mahābhārata.*

As part of the *Bhīṣmaparvan* of the *Mahābhārata,* the *Bhagavadgītā* presents itself as a component of the narrative rather than merely an intrusion, and provides an able synthesis of prevailing religious ideas. But there has been much debate in the past over its relationship to the *Mahābhārata* and over its consistency, with at one stage a strong tendency to dissect the text, particularly by western scholars such as Otto and Jacobi. Hermann Jacobi held the *Bhagavadgītā* to be a later elaboration of the few verses which originally contained Krishna's answer to Arjuna, and isolated this original form as 1.1 - 2.37 (apart from 2.7-8) and 18.73.[1] Rudolf Otto's original *Gītā* contained chs.1; 2.1-13, 20, 22, 29-37; 10.1-8; 11.1-6, 8-12, 14, 17, 19-36, 41-51, and 18.58-61, 66, 72, 73. This "Ur-Text" was expanded by various treatises (Lehrtraktate), of which Otto distinguished eight, each dealing with a specific doctrine and claiming the authority of Krishna as deity.[2] More recently, R Morton Smith has sought by statistical analysis to show that each of three sections is probably by a different author,[3] whereas application of statistical methods to the *śloka* metre reveals for Yardi that, "The *Gītā* is undoubtedly the work of a single author", whom he identifies as Sauti, the third in his series of five authors of the epic.[4] In a more sophisticated analysis, Mislav Jeźic has drawn attention to the repetitions of both meaning and expression, arguing that these help to reveal the structure of the text. On this basis, he distinguishes an epic part of the poem, which then received Yogic and Upanishadic enlargements, a separate hymn in ch.11, and finally a *bhakti* layer which synthesises these.[5]

The tendency to dissect is not, however, confined to western scholars, as is shown by the work, originally in Marāṭhī, of G S Khair, in which he concludes that the *Bhagavadgītā* was composed by three "philosopher-poets" at three different periods. The first, before the 6th century BCE, composed parts of the first six chapters and propounded a theory of yoga and *karma;* the second, about a century later, added the major part of chs.8, 13-15, and 17-18 and incorporated the Sāṃkhya metaphysics; the third, by about the 3rd century BCE recast the whole poem, composing six new chapters (7, 9-12, and 16) and introduced "devotional theism based on the worship of Vāsudeva-Kṛṣṇa".[6]

Equally, though, there have been western scholars who have defended the unity of the *Bhagavadgītā* and argued that it is integral to the *Mahābhārata.* A recent instance is Johanna Sachse,[7] but the most notable, probably, is Paul Oltramare, who affirmed that the *Bhagavadgītā* is there to justify the conduct of the Pāṇḍavas and to enable the *Mahābhārata* to satisfy the requirements of Brahminical morals.[8] As part of his rejection of the possibility that the present text had replaced an original simpler text, he argued that it succeeds in its aim of justifying the heroes' conduct, showing its consistency with Vedic and other schools and opposing those who rejected orthodoxy. Hence it is inappropriate to see it as an insertion. Specifically, he argued that Krishna's instruction is directed precisely at Arjuna's situation, while accepting in effect as its corollary that the text contains views that are logically irreconcilable.[9] Though not persuaded by all the details of his argument, I consider that he has illuminated rather clearly the two views that are in practice tenable about the *Bhagavadgītā:* either it is an integral part of the *Mahābhārata* and directed pragmatically to Arjuna's situation, or it is a later insertion (which includes the possibility of a later expansion of a brief original) developing a philosophically and theologically significant message from its *Mahābhārata* context. One cannot, it seems to me, sensibly regard the *Bhagavadgītā* as both integral to the epic and theologically profound.[10]

Among the reasons for thinking that the *Bhagavadgītā* was not originally part of the *Mahābhārata* is precisely the incongruity of such a sermon at such a point in the narrative. Would both armies really have waited while Krishna answers Arjuna's doubts at such length, especially when the battle has actually begun, as BhG 1.20c indicates *(pravṛtte śastrasampāte)*? There is, of course, the counter-argument that the *Mahābhārata* is not history but dramatic narrative, but this weakens the argument rather than negates it entirely. The contrast between Krishna's revelation of himself as the supreme deity and Arjuna's familiarity with him in the rest of the epic is another argument for the view that the *Bhagavadgītā* is not an original part of the *Mahābhārata.* Nor should we forget, in looking at the *Bhagavadgītā* in its epic context, the repetition, supposedly, of his teaching that Krishna gives to Arjuna after the battle, for the *Anugītā* (Mbh.14.16.50) propounds an appreciably different doctrine, with a strong emphasis on the performance of austerities.

An argument that is sometimes used to prove that the *Bhagavadgītā* is integral to the *Mahābhārata* is drawn from the number of parallels between it and other parts of the epic, with the implicit or explicit assumption that these are quotations of the *Bhagavadgītā.*[11] The situation is in fact more complex. I shall mention later two instances where the *Bhagavadgītā* seems clearly to be borrowing from elsewhere in the *Mahābhārata,* in many more the issue is not clear cut, and there is always the possibility of borrowing from a common source. Often the verses or single lines are not particularly memorable and the identity or close similarity may be due more to the common subject matter than to any specific quoting in either direction.[12] Arguments have also been drawn on a structural basis from, for example, the episode of Śalya acting as Karṇa's charioteer, seen as a kind of inversion, with Śalya's insults a counterpart, even a caricature of Krishna's support of Arjuna.[13]

There are problems too over the *Bhagavadgītā's* relationship to other episodes where Krishna is revealed as divine, such as Draupadī's disrobing at the assembly hall or that earlier theophany in which Krishna reveals himself to Duryodhana (Mbh.5.129.1-15).[14] Perhaps the best response to the first example is along the lines of an article by Madhav Deshpande, where he concludes:

> "The best answer to such a dilemma is provided by the fact that the critical edition of the *Mahābhārata* does not contain this episode, indicating that it must be a later addition to the epic. Thus, it seems likely that elements of Krishna religion were added initially in ways which would keep the logical progression of the *Mahābhārata* story unimpaired. However, in later times, this process of adding elements of Krishna religion continued past a point of maintaining the integrity of the plot of the *Mahābhārata*".[15]

It is, indeed, in my view hardly possible that the *Bhagavadgītā*, at least in its present form, was a part of the original epic narrative and there is clear textual evidence for the process of insertion. In fact, it may well have originated as a separate composition, for it not only presupposes the epic setting, but itself contains a reasonably full description of Arjuna's dilemma (superfluous in its present context but required for an independent work). Georg von Simson has presented evidence for the mechanisms by which the *Bhagavadgītā* was included within the *Mahābhārata*, and has demonstrated that the repetition in Mbh.6.95.4-23 of Mbh.6.16.11-20+42.2 shows that originally the whole block from 16.21 to 42.1 was absent.[16] It is worth noting that this includes most of the more extended *Bhagavadgītāparvan* (Mbh.14-40),[17] where the prediction of Bhīṣma's death and of the mourning for him in some sense provides a specific rationale for Arjuna's revulsion. Indeed, it could be argued that the *Bhagavadgītā* reflects and to that extent was engendered by the shift away from the martial ethos of the early *Mahābhārata* to the more reflective spirit of its later redactors.

Von Simson establishes that there are in fact two stages of interpolation: the first, after 6.16.20, provides the connection between Duryodhana's speech and Duḥśāsana's reaction to it and, through Dhṛtarāṣṭra's question at the end of ch.22, forms a transition to the actual start of the battle at ch.42. At this point, the second stage of interpolation inserts the *Bhagavadgītā* (Mbh.6.23-40) and the visit of the Pāṇḍavas to Bhīṣma and the gurus, before taking up again in 6.42.1 the bridging question by Dhṛtarāṣṭra from the first stage of interpolation. The first insertion (6.16.21-22.22) clearly occurred as part of the great revision of the *Mahābhārata* to which we owe the account of the battle in its present form, whereas the *Bhagavadgītā* reveals itself by its preamble in 1.2-19, which draws on 6.47.2-30, to be later still.[18] Also, in the visit of the Pāṇḍavas to the enemy, which follows the *Bhagavadgītā*, we see a late piece of Brahmin apologetic, which equally with the second visit to Bhīṣma (6.103.40-84) must have been inserted for the moral justification of the Pāṇḍavas.

THE DATE OF THE GĪTĀ

The *Bhagavadgītā* is commonly assigned to about the 2nd century BCE; it is certainly no older, if indeed it is as old as that. This dating seems to be based, on the one hand, on the recognition of its secondary status within the *Mahābhārata*, and on the other hand, on general assumptions about the early development of Vaiṣṇavism. I will turn to the second of these shortly, but first I would like to address the issue of its place in the development of the epic, though in a very tentative fashion, I must confess. My own impression has long been that the *Bhagavadgītā* must be considerably later, more like the first century CE, and one of the reasons for this is the general language and style of the text in relation to the other epic, the *Rāmāyaṇa*. The problem is that little research has been done on this aspect of the *Mahābhārata*, with which comparisons should properly be made, since the style of the two epics is not identical, although the language shows greater similarity. The frequency, for example of the periphrastic future (4 occurrences, equivalent to 1 in every 175 verses), is much closer to that in the *Bāla* and *Uttara kāṇḍas* of the *Rāmāyaṇa* (1 in 180 verses) than to that in the core books (where the proportions range upwards from 1 in over 500 verses). Indeed, its use of the secondary conjugations suggests an even later style than that of the *Bāla* and *Uttara kāṇḍas* (15 desiderative forms, equivalent to 1 in 47 verses, against 1 in 63 in Ram.1+7 and for example, 1 in 78 in Ram.3; 2 intensive forms, as many as in the whole of each of Ram.1-3), although the frequency of the form made with the suffix *-vat* added to the past participle passive is intermediate between the core of the *Rāmāyaṇa* and the *Bāla* and *Uttara kāṇḍas.* This is not the place for listing further such purely linguistic criteria. Suffice it to say that they suggest to me that the *Bhagavadgītā* should be assigned to roughly the same date as the *Bāla* and *Uttara kāṇḍas* of the *Rāmāyaṇa,* which I reckon as the 1st-3rd centuries CE.[19]

The style of the text seems also more consistent with the later epic style, which tends to greater use of poetic devices such as concatenation, anaphora, and the use of refrains, all of which are frequent in the *Bhagavadgītā,* and the piling up of formulaic elements without regard to their aptness. For example, Emeneau has argued that 6.5a-7a (in which forms of *ātman* occur 15 times in these five lines) is predominantly formulaic in character and that "some of it is awkward, if not actually a bad fit in the passage".[20] Vocabulary is not as clear an indicator, although we may note, for example, the prakritic *geha* at 6.41c and the formulation *bhasmasāt kurute* at 4.37b+d (typical in the *Rāmāyaṇa* of the *Bāla* and *Uttara kāṇḍas)* as indicators of a position fairly late in the development of epic Sanskrit, as well as the occurrence of *arthaśāstra* vocabulary: *jigīṣat* at 10.38b and *udāsīna* at 6.9a (imc), 9.9c *(-vat),* 12.16b and 14.23a *(-vat).* Some features, such as *vibhūti* occurring solely in ch.10,[21] are clearly due primarily to the subject matter. It is worth noting, incidentally, that the text nowhere uses the term *līlā* which is so central to the later Krishna cult.

Finally, though much less significantly, a later date of perhaps the first century CE for the *Bhagavadgītā* would have the effect of reducing the enormous time-gap between the text and its first extant commentary by Śaṃkara and thus making that gap less puzzling. Incidentally, the supposed references in the *Bhagavadgītā* and the *Brahmasūtra* to each other are inconclusive: the one reference in the *Bhagavadgītā (brahmasūtrapadaiś caiva,* 13.4c) is not necessarily specifically to Bādarāyaṇa's work, though in my opinion probably so, while the two in the *Brahmasūtra (api smaryate* at 2.3.45, and *smaranti ca,* 4.1.10) could be to any non-Vedic text, and it is only the commentators from Śaṃkara onward who affirm that the *Bhagavadgītā* is meant.

The Gītā in early Vaiṣṇavism

Let me turn now to the place of the *Bhagavadgītā* in early Vaiṣṇavism. We must presume that in the centuries preceding the *Bhagavadgītā,* various cults and beliefs tending towards some kind of monotheism contributed to the rise of Vaiṣṇavism. In the oldest texts of the Vaiṣṇava tradition, the *Mahānārāyaṇa Upaniṣad* and the *Bhagavadgītā,* Viṣṇu himself is only mentioned in passing, in contrast to Nārāyaṇa and Krishna who in the course of time are linked with the Vedic figure who gave his name to the whole tradition. Whereas the slightly older *Mahānārāyaṇa Upaniṣad* makes Nārāyaṇa its supreme being, in the *Bhagavadgītā* Krishna presents himself as the supreme, identical to or more often, superior to Brahman. Viṣṇu's name occurs just three times in the *Bhagavadgītā:* once when Krishna declares that he is Viṣṇu among the Ādityas at 10.21a (but Indra among the gods in the next verse, 10.22b), and twice in the vocative, at 11.24d and 30d,[22] while the name *Hari* is found only at 11.9b and 18.77b. By contrast, the *Nārāyaṇīya,* also included within the *Mahābhārata* (Mbh.12.321-339) and probably no earlier in date than the 3rd century CE, does use the name *Viṣṇu* to designate the supreme deity, mainly in the later chapters (although at 324.30a the Lord is called *Viṣṇu-varada,* "giver of gifts").[23] The tendency to identify various such figures was, however, already visible in the *Śatapatha Brāhmaṇa,* where the Cosmic Person *(Puruṣa)* of *Ṛg Veda* 10.90 is called "Nārāyaṇa" (13.6.1.1)[24] and tends to fuse with Prajāpati, the lord of creatures, who is described as becoming and imitating, that is, identifying himself with Viṣṇu (6.1.1.5, 6.7.2.12ff., 6.7.4.7).

Nārāyaṇa is again central to the *Nārāyaṇīya,* but in general this text propounds a doctrine which, though characterised by *ahiṃsā* (non-violence) and *bhakti* worship of a supreme deity and tending in the direction of the Vāsudeva cult, is not identical with that proclaimed by Krishna in the *Bhagavadgītā.* The *bhakti* of both doctrines is essentially the same but the *Nārāyaṇīya* attaches special value to rites, sacrifices, *tapas* and *yoga.* Whereas the Nārāyaṇa and Bhāgavata religions were probably of different origin, in the course of time they amalgamated. When this combined *bhakti* religion was secondarily absorbed by the broad current of Vaiṣṇavism, Vāsudeva and Nārāyaṇa were, like Krishna of the *Bhagavadgītā,* identified with and sometimes replaced by Viṣṇu. In the *Nārāyaṇīya* the name "Krishna" is not prominent — he is one of the forms of Nārāyaṇa born as Dharma's son (12.321.9) — but Vāsudeva is the central figure of a religion which was explained to his true *bhakta* Nārada (cf.12.332) by Nārāyaṇa himself in Śvetadvīpa: Vāsudeva is the Supreme Soul, the inner ruler of all. His religion is the monotheistic *(ekāntika)* Bhāgavata faith. It is also in the *Nārāyaṇīya* that Bhagavān Nārāyaṇa, the Supreme Soul pervading the entire universe, is considered the promulgator of the Pāñcarātra system (12.337.63ff.). In its devotional aspect, this movement is relatively close to the *Bhagavadgītā*. One feature of the Pāñcarātra lies in its blending with the traditional mythological cult of Viṣṇu's *avatāras* an interpretation which accounts metaphysically for the basic immutability of the supreme god and of his interventions in the universe. The *avatāras* appear as incarnations, often partial, sometimes total, of the divinity for a specific purpose, particularly, as the *Bhagavadgītā* puts it, "when order is breaking down". The need is therefore for the re-establishment of *dharma,* cosmic and moral order — these two aspects being inseparable in Indian thought.

According to the *Nārāyaṇīya,* Nārāyaṇa was born as the son of Dharma in the quadruple form of Nara, Nārāyaṇa, Hari and Krishna (12.321.8-9). Elsewhere, the *Mahābhārata* repeatedly states that Arjuna is Nara and Krishna Vāsudeva is Nārāyaṇa. Nara, the original man, is the son of Indra (Mbh.1.67.110ff.), and their friendship in a sense parallels but inverts the mythical alliance between Indra and Viṣṇu. Nara and Nārāyaṇa are the first two members of the quadruple forms issuing from the One. But the One is also called Nārāyaṇa. The term thus covers two types of reality: one, the supreme deity; the other, one of the manifestations which can be grasped by the senses and human thought, born at the same time as Nara, Hari and Krishna in the house of Dharma, in the *kṛta* age at the start of the cosmic cycle.

The Teaching of the Gītā

The First Six Chapters

As part of one of the epics, the *Bhagavadgītā* falls outside the Vedic literature (though calling itself an *Upaniṣad),* and so has no inherent authority. Yet its setting at the heart of the *Mahābhārata* in fact provides its strength, for Krishna is answering a real-life dilemma for Arjuna and in the process propounds a view of life and a way to liberation with which to a large extent the ordinary person can identify.

The *Bhagavadgītā* thus appeals to those who are still involved in the affairs of the world, just as the *Mahābhārata* as a whole is in a significant sense an enquiry into the nature of *dharma* in all its complexity.

Arjuna's dilemma is that the leaders of the opposing army are his cousins, since the conflict is over possession of their ancestral kingdom. In the first chapter Arjuna gives vent to his despondency and ends up declaring that he will not fight. Thereafter, Krishna shows Arjuna the limitations of his view and stresses the need to fulfil one's role in society. He begins in the second chapter by teaching that the *ātman,* being eternal and indestructible, does not die when the body is killed but transmigrates from body to body until it achieves final release. Thus, death for the *ātman* is impossible, for "just as a man discards worn out clothes and puts on new ones, so the self abandons worn out bodies and acquires other new ones" (2.22).

Quoting from the *Kaṭha Upaniṣad* to reinforce his point, Krishna then applies it to Arjuna's own situation, declaring that since death is not final there is no need for sorrow over the imminent deaths in battle, and he is not averse to including an appeal to Arjuna's fear of being called a coward. It is possible to recognise this eternal *ātman* through the practice of yoga, that is, by learning to detach oneself completely from the results of actions. This leads on through emphasis on the abandoning of desires to declarations that such a person reaches peace and the stillness of Brahman (2.71-72). As this already shows, the *Bhagavadgītā* draws heavily on certain Upaniṣads,[25] as well as other parts of Vedic literature and other less clearly identifiable ways of thinking,[26] although recently it has been argued that the *Śvetāśvatara Upaniṣad* draws on the *Bhagavadgītā* rather than the other way round.[27] It is, indeed, not a completely consistent text but rather it seeks to combine and synthesise into an overall theistic framework the various strands of thought then current. As Julius Lipner has aptly put it, "We may say that it has been the intention of the *BhG* ab initio to incorporate an element of semantic fluidity".[28] It is undoubtedly a work of popularisation and its inclusion in the *Mahābhārata* with its massive audience is not coincidental. Hence the different evaluations of the *Bhagavadgītā:*

> "To put it bluntly, the utility of the *Gītā* derives from its peculiar fundamental defect, namely, dexterity in seeming to reconcile the irreconcilable. The high god repeatedly emphasizes the great virtue of non-killing *(ahiṃsā),* yet the entire discourse is an incentive to war".[29]

> "The Gītā provides a religious justification for continuing an approximately normal human life. Therein lies its strength. It does not ask the impossible and yet it furnishes religious inspiration. It holds out the hope of salvation on terms which are not out of the reach of the great mass of mankind. And it provides for its scheme of salvation a philosophic background, based on commonly accepted Hindu postulates".[30]

To return to the text, in the third chapter Krishna expounds the view that all activity is a sacrifice if undertaken in the right spirit which he goes on to show is one of complete detachment. He thus simultaneously provides a reinterpretation of sacrifice and of the renunciatory way of life. For he makes it clear that withdrawal into inactivity is not only useless but actually misguided, and even hints at insincerity on the part of some renouncers, suggesting that their thoughts may be more worldly than their actions (3.6-7). Just as Krishna, as the supreme deity, has no need to act but is constantly engaged in activity, since otherwise the world would collapse, so one should help to maintain the world order — now by sacrificially-motivated activity rather than the sacrifice itself. This implies a complete change in the idea of sacrifice, which was originally performed with a view to obtaining a desired result but now must be performed without attachment to its "fruit" but "for the good of the worlds". Thus Arjuna should perform his caste duty *(dharma)* of fighting the enemy, but in a spirit of complete detachment without concern for the outcome. In associating himself with Krishna in the battle of *dharma,* Arjuna also becomes the "sacrificer" of this war, he who will ensure the victory of *dharma* and so enable the three worlds to be maintained. Every action becomes a ritual, just as every effort to kill desire becomes a war. Arjuna's action must be an act of yoga, like the act of the supreme deity. Because it is action, his yoga is a *karmayoga,* a yoga of action. But because this action is performed in full awareness of what it has to be, this yoga is also a *jñānayoga,* a yoga of knowledge. Finally, because this disinterested action which runs counter to the warrior's natural feelings is only possible through an unconditional surrender of self to the deity, it is also a *bhaktiyoga,* a yoga of devotion.

The *Bhagavadgītā* thus provides a new aspect to the doctrine of *karman* by stressing the motivation involved. There had already been suggestions in the Upaniṣads that it is desire that leads to actions and this was a prominent feature of the

Buddhist analysis. The *Bhagavadgītā* goes on from this to declare that, since desire is more basic than action, actions as such have no particular effect, provided one acts unselfishly and without interest in the result. In fact, such disinterested action, rather than mere inactivity, is the true opposite to action. Thus renunciation is not the way forward and the *Bhagavadgītā* rejects the practice of asceticism in favour of disciplined activity in the world, suggesting that in any case complete cessation of activity is impossible and the ascetic way of life therefore untenable. Action without attachment is action in accordance with one's *dharma*, one's religious and social duties which vary according to one's particular situation. Thus Arjuna, as a member of the Kṣatriya caste, has a duty to uphold law and order and for that reason to take part in the impending battle. Moreover, Arjuna should not think that he himself is responsible for his actions, for in reality they are performed by the *guṇas*, the constituents of nature, which are entirely separate from the *ātman*.

The commonest meaning of *dharma* in the Dharma Śāstras is the assemblage of duties incumbent on each individual according to his status *(varṇa)* and stage of life *(āśrama)*, to which he must conform. The *Mahābhārata* as a whole takes this understanding of *dharma*, but through the various developments of its plot explores the problems of acting in accordance with *dharma*. To put it rather cynically, it is symptomatic of its approach that Yudhiṣṭhira, who is so often referred to as Dharmarāja, is the least decisive of the five brothers, as Draupadī is ready to point out on various occasions. More charitably, we may accept Greg Bailey's characterisation that Yudhiṣṭhira "embodies a suffering which strongly reflects ascetic values", and so is the most striking example of "the questioning of *dharma* by those who are obliged to uphold it".[31] Perhaps the most striking instance of the ambiguity of *dharma* is the debate over the killing of the four Kaurava generals, but there is much other material pointing to the ambiguity of the concept. Indeed, at such times the epic seems almost to be questioning the validity of the concept as such, while in the didactic material of its 12th and 13th books it expounds its nuances as fully as any Dharma Śāstra. Although this is the approach overall of the developed *Mahābhārata*, it is noteworthy that in one of the frequent formulaic *pādas* (which belong in general to the earlier strata), *sa hi dharmaḥ sanātanaḥ/ eṣa dharmaḥ sanātanaḥ*,[32] the meaning of *dharma* is rather "custom, tradition" — a far cry from the contemporary usage of *sanātana-dharma*.[33]

The sum of the duties incumbent on each individual according to their status and stage of life is basically the meaning of *dharma* in the *Bhagavadgītā* too and notably in that famous passage where Krishna, speaking to Arjuna as he hesitates to fight, says that such is his duty *(sva-dharma)* as a Kṣatriya (2.31).[34] This is in keeping with the traditional theory, which the *Bhagavadgītā* accepts, even devoting several verses to a definitive statement of it (18.41-48), as well as affirming here in the third chapter that one's own duty is better than another's even if badly done (3.35, of which the first line recurs at 18.47ab). However, there are also traces elsewhere in the text of the view that, since all beings are one in god, one should behave in the same way towards all — as one would towards oneself (e.g. 4.35, 5.7, 6.29-32, 13.28).

Thus, since one's own *ātman* is in reality identical with the *ātman* of all other creatures, one who harms others harms himself (as in 13.28), and we must treat all creatures alike, from the highest to the lowest, that is, like ourselves. Truly to apply this moral principle would seem necessarily to rule out any violent injury to living beings, but in the *Bhagavadgītā* the idea of *ahiṃsā* is little developed. The term *ahiṃsā* occurs four times in lists of virtues (10.5a, 13.7b, 16.2a, 17.14c, also *hiṃsā* in 18.25a, 27b) and is never singled out for particular attention, instead being left half hidden in such rather formal lists. But then Krishna's teachings are meant to dispel Arjuna's qualms at killing his opponents, and Arjuna's entirely reasonable question about why one should fight is never fully answered by Krishna. More often the *Bhagavadgītā* does not try to define duty, but contents itself with saying that one should do one's duty simply because it is one's duty — a view that has some similarities with Kant's categorical imperative.

After thus examining the way of action *(karman)* in the third chapter, in the fourth chapter Krishna takes up the way of knowledge *(jñāna)*, the type of intuition going back as far as the speculative hymns of the *Ṛg Veda* but here carefully defined as knowledge of the deity (4.9-10; cf. 7.19, 10.3, 14.1-2). He even claims that knowledge itself may be obtained through disciplined activity (4.38). Interestingly, it is within this chapter that Krishna declares: "Whenever there occurs a decline in righteousness *(dharma)* and a surge in unrighteousness, then I send forth myself, Bhārata. To protect the good and to destroy evil-doers, in order to establish righteousness, I come into being from age to age" (4.7-8). In passing, let me note that the first of these verses is effectively identical to Mbh.3.187.26, within the revelation by Viṣṇu-Nārāyaṇa to Mārkaṇḍeya, into which context it fits more naturally than into the *Bhagavadgītā,* where the passage is concerned mainly with rebirth in general.

However, after such emphasis on the deity come two chapters on Brahman and *ātman* respectively, reverting to ideas of meditation as the means to achieve insight. One explanation that is given for the text's apparent inconsistency is that Krishna seeks to lead Arjuna gradually from a basically atheistic Sāṃkhya-Yoga cosmology and psychology to a fully theistic position. On this view, of the first six chapters three are concerned directly with Brahman and *ātman* and only secondarily with the deity. The soul is by nature an inhabitant of an eternal world, the sum-total of which is termed Brahman, and to become Brahman is to realise eternity. One can recognise this eternal *ātman* here and now through the practice of yoga, that is, by learning to detach oneself completely from the results of action and concentrating one's attention on the deity. However, the deity here is simply the Īśvara or Lord of classical Yoga, the *ātman* totally unaffected by matter which serves as an aid to contemplation.

The theme of Brahman is taken up again in the fifth chapter, which is very similar in its ideas to the second chapter, although its exaltation of Brahman as both the goal of yoga and as an external agency is much more pronounced. It is again concerned with the self-discipline of yoga, which is attained by intense concentration of attention on a single point. Those thus integrated realise that the *ātman* is never the author of any action, for action is the sphere of nature *(svabhāva),* and they experience no emotion, being established in Brahman (5.24). The term *brahmabhūta,* used here (5.24d) and at two other places in the *Bhagavadgītā* (6.27d and 18.54a), occurs several times elsewhere in the *Mahābhārata,* suggesting that these parts perhaps have more in common with other didactic parts of the *Mahābhārata* than some others.[35] At the same time Brahman is the law which operates in nature, for the yogi is told to resign all work to Brahman just as Arjuna was told to leave the deity to do the work (5.10, cf.3.30). But Brahman is both the innermost self *(prabhu,* 5.14) and the pervader of all *(vibhu,* 5.15). There is no mention here of Krishna as deity; indeed, Dhavamony has termed this chapter "a *Brahmavādin*'s interpolation"[36] — while the sixth chapter goes over the same ground yet again but does not equate Brahman with external nature as well as with *ātman.*

Since the first six chapters are mainly devoted to the nature of the *ātman* and the realisation of its timeless essence, it is not surprising that *bhakti* is not prominent. The man of wisdom "has no love *(sneha)* for anything" (2.57): unattached devotion to the deity leads to liberation but not passionate love. Renunciation *(tyāga)* and passionlessness *(vairāgya)* are the ideals and *bhakti* is devotion to the Bhagavat, the Lord, intentness on him with the senses curbed. In fact, *bhakti* is rarely mentioned in these chapters, occurring twice each in the fourth and sixth chapters. At 4.3 Krishna calls Arjuna *bhakta,* since Arjuna trusts his friendly advice and becomes his loyal disciple; at 4.11 Krishna declares that he loves his devotees in the same way as they approach him, but only gradually does Arjuna's *bhakti* develop and become more conscious, for he only realises by stages that his friend and guru is more than a mere man. As one might expect, *bhakti* is absent from the Brahman-orientated fifth chapter, but the sixth chapter strikes a theistic note at its end, and so *bhakti* has its place (6.31 and 47). The yogi's god is at the same time the god of *bhakti,* of the devotion which is an attitude of complete surrender of one's thoughts and acts to the deity (cf.6.46-47, also 4.9-11 and 6.30-31). The transition from yoga to *bhakti* is presented here as a generalisation of yoga. It is a permanent internal attitude, accessible to all.

Incidentally, a strongly divergent view has been presented by John D Smith who argues that "Epic heroes — and by extension we ourselves — are the gods' scapegoats", and who sees a common ideology propounded in both the Sanskrit and the folk epics, which he categorises as "startlingly far-removed from Krishna's celebrated explanation of his own presence on earth" in the *Bhagavadgītā* (4.8) as restorer of *dharma* from age to age.[37] When Krishna tells Arjuna to act without desire for the fruits of his actions, he has base desires of his own in championing the self-interest of the gods.

The Middle Six Chapters

The middle six chapters of the *Bhagavadgītā* then mainly deal with the nature of the supreme deity and his attributes, although the eighth chapter again presents the method of meditation in yoga as the way to release. Even within that chapter, however, the deity is equated with Brahman, the mystical syllable *oṃ* and the supreme *Puruṣa,* or is stated to be superior to Brahman (8.21). As a result, *bhakti* appears most often in chapters 7, 9 and 12, and at the end of chapter 11, where Krishna fully reveals himself as the deity, whereas the eighth chapter refers just twice to *bhakti* in the context of "going to the supreme celestial Person" (8.10) and of gaining the Supreme Person by undivided love (8.22).

Chapter 7 provides a clearly theistic account of Sāṃkhya-Yoga: the eightfold *prakṛti* is called Krishna's "lower nature" (7.4) and also described as his *māyā*, which must be transcended in order to achieve salvation. Krishna's "higher nature" supports or sustains this lower nature, and everything ultimately derives from and dissolves into the higher and lower natures of Krishna (7.5). However, the *Bhagavadgītā* qualifies this semi-pantheism by firmly excluding evil from the deity's nature and, to a passage otherwise suggestive of pantheism (7.8-10), adds the significant verse: "I am the strength of the strong, free from lust and passion; I am desire in (all) beings, (but) not (such desire as is) opposed to *dharma*" (7.11).

Chapter 8 again returns to the yogic theory of achieving an immortal state independent of the deity but, although it repeats much of what precedes, there is a marked difference. Now, even those self-centred yogis who merely use the deity as a focus for their meditation and whose ultimate aim is solely to isolate their own *ātmans* in their eternal essence, will be helped by him and brought near to him in return for their good intentions (8.11-15). Continuing the terminology of the previous chapter, this supreme deity is called both *akṣara*, "imperishable", and *kṣara*, "perishable", and is equated successively with Brahman (8.3), the supreme spirit *(puruṣaḥ paraḥ*, 8.22), and the mystical syllable *oṃ* (8.13).

Emphasis on the deity culminates within this section in the awe-inspiring theophany in the eleventh chapter, where Krishna reveals to Arjuna his universal form (the *viśvarūpadarśana)*, having in the previous chapter identified himself with the most essential aspects of every part of the cosmos. This primeval *Puruṣa* (11.18) is closely associated with terms such as primeval deity, the last prop and resting place of the universe, the highest presence (of divinity) — elsewhere (10.12) associated with the highest Brahman — the one of infinite forms, the knower and what is to be known, the one who has extended, spun, spread and so produced the universe (11.38). This *Puruṣa* is the Cosmic Person of the *Ṛg Veda* 10.90, and implicitly also the sum total of all individual *puruṣas* (8.4), and as such identical with Brahman as propounded in the Upaniṣads. This revelation produces in Arjuna a spirit of humble adoration, summed up as the way of devotion *(bhakti).*

As to what Arjuna saw, it is essentially indescribable, although the passage waxes lyrical in the attempt, making use of more elaborate metres than elsewhere. The vision is described as "made up of all marvels" (11.11c), but we may note the frequency of light imagery, as in the next verse: "If the light of a thousand suns should suddenly burst forth in the sky, that would resemble the brilliance of that great-souled one". At the humblest level this light image is widely spread in the *Mahābhārata* in the simile of the steady lamp applied to the yogi. Elsewhere in the *Bhagavadgītā* we find: "As a lamp stood in a windless place flickers not, this likeness is recorded of the yogi controlled in thought, practising discipline of the self" (6.19).

In form the chapter consists of a hymn in *triṣṭubh*s embedded in introductory and concluding *śloka*s. The style is not particularly different but, while the introductory *śloka*s present the marvellous Glorious Form *(rūpam aiśvaryam)* to us, the hymn confronts us with the Terrible Form *(ghorarūpam).* Krishna's assertion in the hymn that nobody in the human world except Arjuna can see him in this form is most clearly reinterpreted in the concluding *śloka*s as the instruction that there is no other means to see god in this form except through *bhakti.* As Mislav Jeźic has shown, this hymn evidently presupposes the epic part of the text but, since it contains a brief statement of Arjuna's dilemma and not just Krishna's answer to it, it must have been intended as a separate composition and not as another layer added to the epic part.[38] It is indeed worth noting that 12.1 takes up from 10.10, continuing as though the theophany had never happened, just as the rest of the *Mahābhārata* proceeds largely as though the *Bhagavadgītā* were not there.

In her study of the myth of the *pralaya,* Madeleine Biardeau has provided a new perspective with her observation that this chapter — in particular verses 15-33, which comprise Arjuna's description of the vision (15-31) and Krishna's explanation of its meaning (32-33) — is one of two used in the ritual of initiation into *saṃnyāsa.* The choice of BhG 11.15-33 for recitation at this point is significant, for it recalls to the *saṃnyāsin* the cosmic and terrible dimension of the god of *mokṣa,* since the vision which Arjuna has is similar to that which an observer of the *pralaya* would have were he situated beyond it.[39]

The Last Six Chapters

The last six chapters, which are quite probably later in date than the rest, deal with a variety of topics, gradually leading back through a good deal of practical moral teaching (and a summary of Krishna's earlier teaching towards the end of ch.18)[40] to the concept of *bhakti.* Commonly these chapters are accorded very little attention (apart from Krishna's words near the end of ch.18), almost as if they did not really belong to the text. Descriptions here of the Sāṃkhya doctrine conform more closely to the classical scheme than those found in chs. 3 and 7: the passage 13.1-5 gives the classical list of the 25 *tattvas*, while 14.5-21 presents the *guṇas* in the dual role of psychological qualities and constituents of nature *(prakṛti).* The results of the preponderance of each of the three *guṇas* in various parts of *prakṛti* are given in some detail in 14.5-18 (and the whole of ch.17). Most interestingly, in the two preceding verses (14.3-4), cosmic matter is not called *prakṛti* but "great Brahman" and, instead of an evolution of beings out of matter independently of the deity, Krishna plants the germ in the womb of nature. Brahman is probably also an equivalent for material nature in another passage (5.10, cf.above). Thus, in cosmological contexts, Brahman is primal matter, whereas in psychological passages the term is used in the sense of an eternal mode of existence outside time and unaffected by change (as in *brahmanirvāṇa, brahmabhūta* etc.), the realisation of immortality.

At 15.16, the text speaks of two *puruṣas (dvau puruṣau),* one perishable, the other imperishable, and explains: the perishable is all beings, the imperishable is called the one who is aloof or sublime *(kūṭastha).* This passage has often been discussed,[41] but clearly the imperishable is that aspect which may be called the sum total of all liberated selves and the perishable *puruṣa* is the person bound to material nature. Zaehner regards the term *kūṭastha* as due to Buddhist influence, since the equivalent *kūṭattho* is found in the Pali canon, as Renou had earlier noted.[42] The term occurs three times in the *Bhagavadgītā.* It refers either to the released individual, as at 6.8, or to the general state shared by all such released individuals, as here, where the one "standing on the peak" is the imperishable person, the Brahman-Ātman as eternal, changeless being. At 6.8 it is used of the man who has achieved a serene indifference, the equanimity characteristic of Brahman itself, and describes the total detachment of the true self from all that is other than the self. It also occurs at 12.3

— 4 where the "imperishable unmanifest" must also be the aggregate of released selves — the unchanging essence in all described already in 2.24-5 in almost identical terms. Krishna is thus declaring that those who concentrate on the eternal essence within themselves must reach his own being, since he is the source of eternity itself (cf.15.17). Elsewhere in the *Mahābhārata*, in a basically Sāṃkhya context, the wise man who knows the imperishable as aloof, *kūṭastha*, reaches the imperishable Brahman and is freed from *saṃsāra* (Mbh.12.231.34). In the verse, 15.17, Krishna adds: "But there is (yet) another Person [i.e. a third one, or rather a third aspect of the Puruṣa concept], the sublime *(uttama)*, also named the supreme *(parama) ātman*, who enters and pervades the three worlds, sustaining them, the imperishable Lord". Krishna here, while claiming these titles, is clearly denying them to the second aspect of the *puruṣa*, the liberated soul.

The gradual return to the concept of *bhakti* culminates with the declaration, at the end of the whole poem, of Krishna's attachment *(bhakti)* to Arjuna and the promise that by his grace he can be reached and entered into. The nature of this devotion in the *Bhagavadgītā* is rather different from later views; sacrifice and discipline are its hallmarks and there is little room for spontaneity. Indeed, the stress on duty *(dharma)* as specifically the role appropriate to one's station in life leads in the opposite direction. Nor is there any real suggestion of intimacy, except as part of the goal, but rather the attitude of the devotee is one of subservience, typified by Arjuna's humble response to Krishna's divine self-revelation. This way of devotion, available to all, is ranked higher than the way of knowledge, which because of its difficulties only a few can achieve, and that in turn is superior to the way of action, the performance of deeds without attachment to their results but merely out of duty. These ways are not rejected, but a definite order of value is established; this is perhaps the first clear appearance of this principle of ranking. More importantly still, by its stress on the happiness secured by detachment here and now, the *Bhagavadgītā* begins the shift of emphasis in the theistic strands of Hinduism away from the idea of release *(mokṣa)* in some distant future to an immediate and direct relationship with the deity. In this as in much else, the *Bhagavadgītā* stands at the very beginning of what is a long process of development.

1 H Jacobi, 1918: 323-327.
2 See R Otto, 1934, and 1935.
3 R Morton Smith, 1968: 39-46. The three sections are chs.1-12 plus ch.18.55-78; chs.13-16; and chs.17.1-18.54. He also suspected that 2.19-20, 28-29 and 3.23cd were interpolated, and that ch.10 had been modified. Smith counted the ratios of declined stems, of nominal compounds and of particles, to lines.
4 M R Yardi, 1991 (quoting p.5). Incidentally, Yardi dates the *Bhagavadgītā* to around 450 BCE.
5 1986: 628-638, and 1979: 545-557.
6 G S Khair, 1969. Another such attempt is that by Purushottam Lal Bhargava, 1977: 357-71. This sees the *Bhagavadgītā* as consisting of "two clear-cut parts" — a later part in which Krishna claims to be god, consisting of chs.7-12, and the earlier part consisting of the other twelve chapters (with some minor exceptions — verses also claiming divinity for Krishna, which he argues are clearly interpolated).
7 J Sachse, 1988. She argues basically that the author or redactor gave his yoga ideas a Brahminic flavour by introducing the teaching concerning sacrifice, which readers who did not understand the metaphor involved could take literally.
8 P Oltramare, 1928: 161-185. Cf. also his article, 1925: 69-75, where he sees the *Mahābhārata* as witnessing to the struggle between the older philosophical ideas, found in the early Upaniṣads and in the orthodox systems, and the sectarian spirit of devotion, and regards it as centring on the theme of *dharma.*
9 "Mais si la Bhagavad-Gītā n'est proprement l'exposé ni du Vedānta, ni du Sāṃkhya, ni du Bhaktimārga, si elle est ce qu'elle prétend être, une justification du dharma, et tout particulièrement du dharma des kṣatriyas, tous ces philosophèmes n'ont plus qu'une valeur secondaire; il ne sont pas là pour eux, mais servent à la démonstration de la thèse principale.....La Bhagavad-Gītā aussi accepte et même soutient des dogmes logiquement inconciliables, pourvu que les obligations de la caste soient maintenues et respectées", op.cit., p. 180.
10 The suggestion recently put forward by Milton Eder, 1988: 133-143, of approaching the text "as a collection of arguments, arguments encased within chapters which are internally consistent without concern for statements taken from different parts of the text", does not, I think, affect this.
11 For example, Robert N Minor states with more finesse than most: "Finally one must note that complete verses and partial verses from the *Gītā* are quoted verbatim throughout the Epic.....That the *Gītā* is referred to in the Mahābhārata, however, does not show that the *Gītā* was originally a part of the Epic, but it does argue that these portions of the Epic are later than the *Gītā's* addition to it"; 1982: pp.xxix-xxxi.
12 For the record, instances that I have noted are as follows (identity of single *pādas* has usually been ignored as due either to the formulaic nature of the epic style or to coincidence; asterisks refer to verses not in the text but in the critical apparatus): 1.2-19 is very similar to 6.47.2-30, 2.28 cf.11.7*1-2, 2.31cd cf.6.118.32cd, 2.37ab cf.4.64.25cd, 2.38ab is very similar to 12.277.37ab, 2.46 to 5.45.23, 2.58ab to 12.21.3ab and 168.40ab, 2.70 cf. 12.243.9 + 693*, 3.24ab cf. 3.33.10ab, 3.42 cf. 12.238.3, 4.7 is very similar to 3.187.26, 5.5 cf. 12.304.4, also 12.293.30, 5.18 is very similar to 12.231.19, 5.20ab cf. 3.198.41ab and 12.170.5cd, 6.5cd is identical to 5.34.62cd and 13.6.27ab (cf.11.11*3), 6.22ab is very similar to 13.16.42ab, 6.23ab cf. 3.203.44cd, 6.29ab is very similar to 12.313.29ab, 9.32bcd is identical to 14.19.56bcd, 9.33a is very similar to 14.19.57a, 11.11ab is identical (apart from case) to 13.110.97cd, 123ab; 11.22ab is very similar to 13.143.32ab, 12.15ab cf. 14.46.39ab, 13.13 is identical to 12.231.29 and 291.16 (also to Svet.Up. 3.16), 13.30 is identical to 12.17.22, 14.18 is very similar to 14.39.10, 14.24 to 12.679* 1-2, 17.2cd to 12.187.28cd and 336.63cd, 17.3cd is identical to 12.256.14cd, 17.14cd to 12.210.17ab, 18.14 is very similar to 12.898*, 18.41ab is identical to 12.108.1ab, and 18.72ab is very similar to 14.19.50ab.
13 Walter Ruben, 1944: 221, and Alf Hiltebeitel, 1976: 255-9.
14 On the second of these, see R Otto op.cit., and A Hiltebeitel, op.cit., pp.120-8 and 139.
15 Madhav M Deshpande in A Sharma (ed.), 1991: 334-48 (quote from p.348), reprinted from *Journal of South Asian Literature* 23.2, 1988, pp.133-43, with a new conclusion.
16 G von Simson, 1969: 159-74.
17 J A B van Buitenen is unique in translating this larger unit in his work: 1981.
18 On this point, besides von Simson's article, see J A B van Buitenen, 1965: 99-109, esp. p.102.
19 See my *Righteous Rāma,* Delhi, 1984, especially ch.2. The *Bhagavadgītā* data come from my own collection, checked against the word-index prepared by Peter Schreiner. I am much indebted to him for making it available to me, as well as for comments on this paper.
20 M B Emeneau, 1968: 269-278 (quoting p.273). Emeneau affirmed that "even such an incomplete collection as I have at hand shows that more than two-thirds of the material in the first two verses of the passage is formulaic". To his data should be added the fact that 6.5b is identical to Mbh.12.128.17d.
21 At 10.7a, 16bc, 18b, 19b, 40bd, and 41a (*-mat*).
22 Final vocatives such as these are, of course, prime examples of "*pāda*-fillers" which have no essential connection with the rest of the verse, and can easily be substituted one for another. Two other epithets used of Krishna in the *Bhagavadgītā* are "Madhusūdana" at 1.35b; 2.1d, 4b; 6.33b; and 8.2b (all except the occurrence at 2.1d in the vocative), and "Janārdana" at 1.36b, 39d, 44b; 3.1b; 10.18b; and 11.51d. Both are used elsewhere in the *Mahābhārata* and in later texts still, to refer to Viṣṇu as well as to Krishna. However, the existence of an Asura named "Madhu", whose son Lavaṇa is killed by Śatrughna in the *Uttarakāṇḍa* of the *Rāmāyaṇa,* hardly suggests that there is any specific reference yet to Viṣṇu.
23 His absolute superiority is proclaimed at 328.26ab: "Viṣṇu does not bow before any other deity than himself". Thereafter,

the name *Viṣṇu* is often used instead of *Nārāyaṇa,* although in 12.329 it is most frequent in the prose portion, which seems late in character, being almost Purāṇic. See Anne-Marie Esnoul, 1979: 10.

24 Traditionally Nārāyaṇa is the seer or poet of this hymn — perhaps a case of a historical or legendary founder of a religious movement who becomes identified with the deity he preached.

25 Compare 8.11 with Kaṭha Up.2.15; 2.19-20 with Kaṭha.Up.2.18-19; 2.29 with Kaṭha Up.2.7; 3.42 with Kaṭha Up.3.10; 15.6 with Kaṭha Up.5.15; 13.15 with Īśa Up.5, and 13.16a with BĀUp.4.4.17, and 13.16b with Muṇḍ.Up.2.2.6; also, for the image of the Aśvattha tree, see Kaṭha Up.6 init. and Śve.Up.3.9. The number of quotations shows that the *Bhagavadgītā* is deliberately using them for their prestige value, and that it was composed at a period when these Upaniṣads were regarded as authoritative. See also Alf Hiltebeitel, 1984-5: 1-26.

26 Probably too ambitiously Richard V De Smet, 1975: 1-30, affirms that the *Bhagavadgītā* blends elements from nine traditions: ritualistic Brahminism, Upanishadic doctrines, early Sāṃkhya, Yoga, Śaivism, the Nārāyaṇa-Viṣṇu cult, the Vāsudeva-Krishna cult, Jainism and Buddhism. We may, however, note the use of Mīmāṃsā vocabulary (*adhikāra* at 2.47a and, less distinctively, *pātra* and *apātra* at 17.20c and 22b, and *saṃkalpa* at 4.19b, 6.2c, 4c, 24a), as well as other terms from the ritual tradition (e.g. *purodhas* at 10.24a). More philosophical terms include *adhidaivata* at 8.4b, and *adhibhūta* at 7.30a and 8.1a, 4a, as well as the frequent *adhyātma:* 3.30d; 7.29d; 8.1a, 3b; 10.32c; 11.1b; 13.11a and 15.5a.

27 Thomas Oberlies has tentatively concluded that the *Bhagavadgītā* should be regarded as earlier than the *Śvetāśvatara Upaniṣad,* which he assigns to the 1st-2nd century CE; 1988: 35-62, esp.pp.57-9, and 1995: 61-102. Cf. BhG.5.13c with Śvet.Up.3.18a; 8.9d with Śvet.Up.3.8b; 13.13-14ab with Śvet.Up.3.16-17ab (both based on RV 10.81.3, just as the previous verse in Śvet.Up. is identical to RV 10.90.2) and 13.16d with Śvet.Up.3.13/4.20.

28 Julius J Lipner, 1987: 54-73 (quoting p.69). He particularly notes the varying meanings of the term *brahman* within the text.

29 D D Kosambi, 1961: 198-224 (quoting p.206). Cf. Greg Bailey, 1984: 343-353.

30 F Edgerton, 1944: 57.

31 G M Bailey, 1983: 109-129 (quoting pp.119 and 124).

32 Viz. a reference to "the eternal *dharma*"; *sa hi dharmaḥ sanātanaḥ* occurs at Mbh.1.113.7d; 3.86.21d; 5.83.7b, and 15.26.19b (also *Rāmāyaṇa* 2.152d, 21.10d, and 27.30d), and *eṣa dharmaḥ sanātanaḥ* at Mbh.1.113.13d; 3.13.6d, 30.50b, 152.9b, 281.20d; 4.50.7d; 12.96.13f, 128.30d, 131.2d, 298.9d; 13.44.32d, 96.46d, and 14.50.37b (also Rām.1.24.16b, 3.3.24b, and 5.1.100b). Cf. also *naiṣa dharmaḥ sanātanaḥ,* Mbh.1.158.20d; 5.86.17d; 9.30.12b, and 12.259.12b, and *na sa dharmaḥ sanātanaḥ,* Mbh.12.139.70b.

33 The centrality of *dharma* as a theme of the epic has been the focus of a number of recent studies, or at least a major component of them. Examples are Alf Hiltebeitel's already cited work; N Klaes, 1975; and B Matilal (ed.), 1989.

34 However, according to Francis X D'Sa, 1980: 335-357, the *Bhagavadgītā* protests against the usual interpretation of *dharma* as *kula-dharma,* and in effect gives it a cosmic dimension.

35 The term occurs at Mbh.1.1.12d; 3.82.58d, 145.30c, 181.12c, 202.14c; 6.63.16a, 64.1b; 7.172.55b; 12.49.19b, 192.122c, 210.28c, 316.52a; 13.26.41f., 56.17c, 118.7a, 119.22d, and 14.26.26c (also, incidentally, at Rām.1.32.16b). Similarly, *brahmabhūyāya kalpate* at BhG.14.26d and 18.53d occurs also at Mbh.12.154.25d, 208.19d, 243.7d; 12.138.31d, 130.33d, 131.56d, and 14.47.8d. I would therefore disagree with Zaehner's assertion that "the phrase *brahma-bhūta,* "become Brahman", seems to have been borrowed from Buddhism", 1969: 29; see also pp.10-11 and 214. See also Michael McElvaney, in Y Williams and M McElvaney (eds.), 1988: p.28.

36 M Dhavamony, 1971: 77: "If the fifth chapter is a *Brahmavādin*'s interpolation, then *bhakti* should be absent from it, and actually it is not even once mentioned in it".

37 John D Smith in Stuart H Blackburn et al (eds.), 1989: 176-194 (quoting pp.193 and 176).

38 M Ježic, 1986: 628-38.

39 M Biardeau, 1971: 17-89. See also A Hiltebeitel, 1976: 114-20.

40 Some of this recapitulation actually echoes the wording of earlier chapters: 18.37 combines 3.35ab and 4.21cd; 53ab is similar to 16.18ab, and 65ab is identical to 9.34ab (the identity extending into the third *pāda).*

41 For example, in E H Johnston, 1937: 74-5.

42 R C Zaehner, 1967: 381-7, esp. p.382; and L Renou, 1951: 25.

Upholding the World: Dharma in the Bhagavadgītā[1]

4

JACQUELINE HIRST

THREE ISSUES AND QUESTIONS OF PROCEDURE

On the face of it, the issue of *dharma* in the *Bhagavadgītā* is remarkably simple. Arjuna faces a moral dilemma, a pair of "dharmic pulls"[2] between clan duty *(kula-dharma)* and warrior duty *(kṣatriya-dharma),* in which following the latter seems to involve destroying the former and with it the whole social fabric (1.28-46). Krishna gives him a new context in which to assess his apparent dilemma (the self does not really slay nor is it slain, 2.19f., so act with detachment, 2.47), and a quite straightforward teaching: it is better to perform your own *dharma* imperfectly than another's well (3.35). The dilemma is dissolved. A clear course of action emerges (and is, indeed, followed). End of story, since the recommendation is reiterated in ch.18 (especially 18.43-48). It appears that Gandhi could have been right in suggesting that the *Gītā* could have ended with ch.3, the rest being elaboration.[3]

However, this does not even begin to tackle three central issues which are necessarily raised by the current context of this exploration of *dharma* in the *Gītā*.[4] The first is about the nature, content and structure of the text itself. Is it the case that *dharma* is of significance only at the beginning and end of the *Gītā*, perhaps to make a link with the undoubted concerns of the *Mahābhārata* and the battle in particular? Or does such a reading ignore vital clues in the text that a reorientation of *dharma* is taking place, a process which does not involve Arjuna alone? To put it another way, according to the *Gītā* how *is* the world upheld?

The second issue stems from this. Who is involved in upholding the world in "our times"? What is our part in this venture? This raises enormous questions about the nature of the academy and its relationship to the communities it studies. It would be quite wrong to insinuate that the *Bhagavadgītā* was an insignificant text before the interaction of Europe and India in the modern period. Its place in the triple foundation of Vedānta is clear and it acted as a model for other texts, the *Īśvaragītā* being one example. However, its prominence in neo-Hindu thought in the nineteenth and twentieth centuries cannot be abstracted from a context in which western academics stressed the textual basis of religions, Christian missionaries preached on social ethics and Hindu Indian nationalists looked for inspiration to their own heritage as justification for diverse approaches to obtaining Independence.[5] With such a background in mind, it is not possible to explore ways of upholding the world in our times in relation to a particular text, the *Bhagavadgītā*, without raising questions about intentions, foundations, boundaries, knowledge and power. These are, however, I contend, entailed in the study of *dharma* itself.[6]

The third issue, once again, follows. To what extent are the "fruits of our desiring" shaped by what it is *we* desire, our interpretations by our ends? The radically different interpretations of a Śaṃkara and a Rāmānuja, a Tilak and a Gandhi, a Śivānanda and a Prabhupāda, have different fruits in mind and, with them, different assessments of *dharma*, its significance and scope. Yet they share a universe of discourse, a soteriological and/or ethical aim, a search for truth which rejects the misconstructions of others. It is a matter for discussion to what extent and in what context this is also the western academic's aim.[7]

Difficulties similar to those involved here were highlighted in reactions to Peter Brook's film-version of the *Mahābhārata*. While some critics felt that Brook's company had achieved an apt recasting of this story for a western audience,[8] others accused him of cultural plundering and of perpetuating orientalist discourse.[9] A substantive aspect of this latter criticism was the charge that, without an articulation of the framework of *dharma* and indeed of rebirth, the characters, their concerns and reactions were trivialised. The universal story failed, according to such critics, because it was no longer true to the particular.

In the exploration which follows, I have tried to be true to various particulars: to structures in the *Gītā* text, to a recognition that my detection of such structures reflects but also reshapes my own concerns, to a view that acknowledgement of difference may be at least as important as acceptance of commonality. I accordingly hold that I do others a disservice if I assume either that the world I uphold is just the same as theirs or if I assume that they are radically incommensurable, and I have tried to listen to what the *Gītā* might have to say to this prejudice.

My method in this paper will be to focus on three key moments in the *Gītā* to see what light these throw on our reflections on *dharma.* The three moments are: (i) the very opening of the *Gītā* on the *dharma* field, (ii) its process of reinterpreting what is to be considered dharmic, and (iii) Krishna's encouragement to give up all *dharma*s towards the end of ch.18.[10] I shall consider these moments in three stages. The first will give an exegesis of *dharma* in the text itself, a presentation which will, of course, reflect my own interpretative choices. The second will revisit the three moments briefly, in the light of some modern interpretations. The third will use those moments to draw together some reflections on our theme. These reflections will try to incorporate points raised in discussion amongst participants at the Inaugural Conference. This represents an attempt to remain true to my rejection of a straightforward model of transmission from academy to community, a rejection which this paper is partly designed to articulate.With that in mind, we turn to the *Gītā* itself.

For the purposes of this exploration, I shall adopt the following positions. I shall approach the *Gītā* as a unitary text of eighteen chapters, which is to be read cumulatively. On such a reading, contradictory statements need not indicate inconsistency or textual additions, but can be seen as part of a process of understanding which drives Arjuna and the reader on beyond initial preconceptions. I take this position for the following reasons: it acknowledges the way the text has been commented on in the Vedānta traditions; it seems to make good sense of the dynamics and structure of the text itself,[11] in particular its pedagogic method; and it will provide the basis for my final reflections, in which the questions raised by myself and other participants will be crucial in considering "for our times", the nature of the *dharma* field, what is dharmic, and what is to be left behind.

I shall also consider the *Gītā* as a text which, though complete in itself in many ways, needs to be heard in its wider context in the *Mahābhārata* as well as in its clear self-referencing to certain principal Upaniṣads.[12] Further, I assume that Halbfass' comments about the xenology of pre-modern Indian traditions apply to the *Bhagavadgītā* itself, despite modern universalising readings of it.[13] In such a world-view, those beyond the scope of *varnāśrama-dharma* are simply not considered as "others" in the light of whom one can understand oneself. Indeed, so far as the *Gītā* is concerned, they do not exist.[14] However, this raises crucial questions about how its worldview is to be applied in a pluralist/secularist/communalist world. That too is an issue of *dharma*. Finally, though the focus of this paper is necessarily on a text, it seems important to point out that for many Hindus their understanding of *dharma* is not derived directly from the *Gītā* nor indeed from any particular (written) text.[15] To construe this as a weakness is to participate precisely in that "control of knowledge"[16] of which, I have suggested, we should be suspicious. With questions thus raised about our own roles, we contemplate the *dharma* field.

(I) On the Dharma Field

Arjuna's dilemma is articulated, as the text says in its opening verse, "on the field of *dharma*, the field of the Kurus" *(dharmakṣetre kurukṣetre;* 1.1). This is the actual battlefield on which, in alliances, the kings of the known world are involved in a war between those who share a close and common ancestry. It is the Kurukṣetra. Yet, as the field of *dharma*, this is not just a human battle, but one of cosmic proportions.[17] Chapter 11 will leave us in no doubt about the cosmic dimension of the *Gītā's* vision (though the Yuga framework is not explicit here). Perhaps, as importantly, the phrase signals that the *scope* and *nature* of *dharma* will be at issue here. The struggle concerns *dharma* itself. The phrase may also hint already at the teaching of ch. 13 that knowledge is knowledge of the *field* (the realm of *prakṛti*, mind-matter) and of the knower of the field *(puruṣa, ātman,* true self). *Dharma* requires understanding. "That which is called Kurukṣetra is the field causing growth of *dharma* and understanding of it", says Ānandagiri in his gloss of 1.1.[18] As Biardeau observes in a more general context, the concept of *dharma* has resonances at many different levels.[19] The *Gītā's* use seems to be no exception here. It is on this field that we hear Arjuna's original perception of the connection between social and ritual order and the *dharmas* of clan and birth group. He starts very close to home in his dharmic preoccupations, though the implications for him of neglecting these observances are, literally, world-shattering. But this brings us to our second moment, the transformation of understandings of the dharmic.

(II) What is dharmic?

Krishna's response to Arjuna's fears in chs. 2 and 3 is well-known. As we have seen, what Krishna does is to offer Arjuna another, detached perspective: the self neither slays nor is slain (2.19f), action belongs to the *guṇas* and so proper action is action detached from its results (cf.2.47). With it goes an apparently unambiguous definition of *dharma* and hence right action. This is *sva-dharma,* identified for Arjuna as *kṣatriya-dharma,* the duties of the warrior, the social group to which he belongs by birth[20] — "Better to die doing one's own *dharma* even if of poor quality *(viguṇaḥ)* than to do another's well", paraphrasing 3.35.

However, crucially, this *varṇa-dharma* has to be understood in relation to the way Krishna upholds the world: as source of the order which maintains macrocosm and microcosm, as the one who continually effects that order through the workings of *prakṛti,* as the one who takes human form age by age to re-establish *dharma* when it is on the decline. In numerous ways, Krishna's teaching shows how earlier views of order in the universe are taken up and transmuted in understanding who Krishna really is, not least as the one who taught this yoga from the very beginning to Vivasvat, father of Manu, the eponymous ancestor of humans (4.1). Order in human society is, from the beginning, grounded in cosmic order and taught as such.

I will give just one example. In the Vedic *Saṃhitās*, order is maintained by the sacrifice *(yajña),* a mesocosm or link between the macrocosm (the world out there, *adhidaiva,* what pertains to the *devas*; *adhibhūta,* what pertains to the elements common to the whole cosmos), and the microcosm (the world of the sacrificer, the individual if you like, the *adhyātma,* what pertains to the self).[21] The Upaniṣads then pursue a search for the reality underlying both macrocosm and microcosm, a reality variously called *brahman, ātman, puruṣa* and so on. Now in the *Gītā,* those who take refuge in Krishna know the following (see 8.3-4): the supreme imperishable

Brahman, *karman* which is the creative force bringing all beings into existence,[22] the *adhyātma* pertaining to one's own nature *(svabhāva),* Krishna along with the *adhibhūta* (now perishable existence), the *adhidaiva* (now the *puruṣa,* indwelling consciousness), and the *adhiyajña* (realm of sacrifice).

Here is a clear and self-conscious example of the *Gītā's* pedagogical method of reinterpreting and drawing into a new context earlier terms. Krishna answers Arjuna's naive but persistent questions on definitions with responses which are based on a deeper teaching already implied but not yet fully understood. In this case, all the previously discovered principles of order (sacrifice, microcosm, and macrocosm; *brahman; karman)* are understood in knowing Krishna and in relation to Krishna. Krishna subsumes them all. He is both sacrifice (9.16) and enjoyer of sacrifices (5.29), the one in whom order is grounded and who operates the constructing system of *karman* and its results through the three constituents of *prakṛti* (7.12f.). This material nature is his lower nature, *puruṣa,* collective principles of consciousness (and I think they are plural in the *Gītā),* abiding in his higher one. The one who knows all this comes to Krishna at death (7.30), that is, is precisely freed from the structuring mechanisms which maintain the world of *saṃsāra.* Further, sacrifice is now understood as dedicating one's actions to Krishna, so that, even within this world, no further binding constructions are being created. This is a radical reinterpretation. The prime constructor of worlds — sacrifice — reinterpreted, no longer constructs a future of rebirths, but is still fundamentally concerned with "upholding the world", as we shall see.

In the preceding section, the word *dharma* was not mentioned as such. However, earlier in ch.7, Krishna says quite clearly:

> "By this [Krishna's higher nature, *puruṣa*], this universe is upheld *(dhāryate).* Understand clearly *(upadhāraya* — surely a conscious use) that all beings have their wombs in this [higher and possibly, lower nature]. I [Krishna identified in 7.10 with the "seed"] am the origin and also the dissolution of the whole universe (7.5-6) .....On Me all this universe is strung like pearls on a thread" (7.7).[23]

Krishna is thus plainly shown to be the ground of what upholds the universe and, because of this, his yoga in manifesting and sustaining the universe becomes of interest to us.

In particular, Krishna is the one who continually constructs the social order of the four *varṇas* according to people's actions and qualities (4.13),[24] *varṇas* into which people are born in accordance, it seems, with their ritual actions (4.12). Yet Krishna is unattached to the results of his action in this. So he offers himself as a model for the detached action of others (3.21f), perhaps subtly inverting the Dharma Śāstra's usual order of the sources of *dharma: śruti, smṛti,* the conduct of the learned (in the Vedas), and "one's own inner inclination".[25] Now the prime source of *dharma* is Krishna's conduct, not because he is learned in the Vedas (of what use is a tank of water when there are floods all around, asks the *Gītā,* see 2.45-6), but because he is the very source of *dharma* itself. By following Krishna's example of detached action, the wise will continue to uphold the world, to act for *lokasaṃgraha,* the welfare or holding together of the world. Were Krishna not to give this example, people would neglect to act properly and chaos would ensue (3.23-25).

The order which is to be maintained was expressed by the Vedas in sacrificial ritual, but now needs understanding in its proper context. Such is the understanding which Krishna has taught humanity since the beginning of each age. In freely chosen human form he comes again to teach this yoga (4.6f), a detached method of acting, which becomes itself both method and content of what he teaches. It is this whole teaching which is deemed the "most secret.....knowledge of kings [or kingly knowledge — note, Arjuna, its value]. It is *dharmyam,* easy to carry out, imperishable" (9.1-2).

Knowing it, Arjuna will be liberated *(mokṣyase)* from impurity. However, those without faith in this *dharma* will not come to Krishna, but are on the path of the perpetual cycle of deaths (9.3). Perhaps Sargeant is not as mischievous as would appear when he translates *dharma* in his word by word version of 9.3, literally, as "law", but then in the full translation gives it as "worship". For it is worship of Krishna which the chapter goes on to recommend in its famous verse:

> "The one who offers to me with devotion a leaf, flower, fruit or water, I accept that offering of devotion from one who dedicates himself" (9.26).[26]

Once again, this comes in the context of redefining sacrifices, of seeing Krishna as their true recipient and all one's thoughts and actions as the appropriately targeted gift *(arpaṇa,* 9.27). It is this which is truly dharmic.

This seems a long way from Arjuna's concerns with clan and birth-group customs or even Krishna's own advice to follow his *kṣatriya-dharma.* Yet the climactic ch.11, in which Krishna displays his celestial form, returns us to the theme. For Krishna, having shown himself as time devouring the warriors of the battlefield, urges Arjuna to fight (11.32-4). The vision shows Krishna to be the resting place of the universe, the eternal *(sanātana) puruṣa,* the imperishable protector of the everlasting *(śāśvata) dharma,* the cosmic order which must be maintained (11.18). Arjuna can either be dragged along into the cosmic conflagration because of his very make-up, a make-up which is his by karmic inheritance and is in accordance with the cosmic and social order which Krishna constructs, or he can model his freely chosen detached action on Krishna's, knowing him as he really is.

Perhaps, though, I have prejudged the meaning of that phrase used almost in passing: *śāśvata-dharma,* the everlasting *dharma(s)* which the eternal Krishna protects. I have just suggested that it is the cosmic order (singular) which is concerned here. But this raises the question of its relation to the age-old customs of clans (plural), which were Arjuna's starting-point, and to *varṇa-dharma* (singular and plural) constructed according to (ritual and other) activity and constructing the world in turn. The imperishable dharmic knowledge (9.1-2) was about detachment from such action, properly expressed by the dedication of all worship to Krishna. But though ritual activity may be satisfied by the simple offering of a flower, this does not necessarily entail the neglect of other *dharmas*; indeed such renunciation is quite clearly rejected (18.5f). The world is still to be upheld by the detached performance of what is dharmic, following the example of Krishna's own yoga. Perhaps this phrase *śāśvata-dharma,* then, in its simple solidity, unites all fragmented understandings of *dharma* in a single ground.

There are other possibilities, however. It may ask us, like Arjuna, to go beyond our initial understandings of *dharma,* discarding or recontextualising them as we go, to that which is truly dharmic. Or maybe it just indicates the difficulties of reading the *Gītā* as a coherent whole, its various understandings of *dharma,* perhaps like ours, left unresolved. Finally, its complex simplicity may warn us of the danger of assuming the normativity of any one of the fragmentary meanings, apart from that which grounds it. We turn to the final moment.

The Renunciation of Dharmas

In chapter 18, after recapitulating quite clearly the link between actions specific to different *varṇas* and paricular prākṛtic make-ups, Krishna finally advises Arjuna:

> "Having renounced all *dharmas (sarvadharmān parityajya),* come to Me as your only refuge. I will liberate you from all demerits *(sarvapāpebhyaḥ).* Do not grieve." (18.66)

This verse is a gift to Śaṃkara, the great Advaitin thinker. He sees it as a plain indication that all actions, whether dharmic or adharmic, are to be given up in favour of knowledge of the Self.[27] Rāmānuja pays more heed to the *Gītā's* own distinction between *saṃnyāsa* (ascetic renunciation) and *tyāga* (renunciation of results). He advises that it is the whole trio of the fruits of *dharmas* (understood as *karmayoga, jñānayoga* and *bhaktiyoga,* performed as aspects of worshipping Krishna), actions and one's own sense of agency, which are to be left behind, for they are simply means to the highest bliss.[28] Krishna — the only refuge and goal.

In terms of the structure of the *Gītā,* we might also see this rejection as a turning away from those initial concerns of clan and birth-group customs and from the results of a person's own *kṣatriya-* or whatever *dharma,* and from the grief of attachment, whether by liking or hatred, for a given role. This would accord with an understanding of the text which moves Arjuna away from his initial preoccupations, transforming his view of what is dharmic. But if the key to this transformation is one's attitude, this could, after all, be seen to favour an interpretation which reinforces the particular *dharmas,* though to be performed with suitable detachment. While few of the modern commentators I have consulted make much of this verse (Radhakrishnan is an exception), questions about the nature of *sva-dharma* and attitudes to it are one of their pivotal concerns. At this point, then, we shall revisit our three moments in the light of modern interpretations.

Modern Interpretations

First, we go back to the battlefield, the field of *dharma,* and find that for Gandhi, addressing the members of Sabarmati ashram in 1926, it has become the body with personified forces struggling within each of us: "It is the human body that is described as Kurukshetra, as *dharmakshetra.* It does become that when used in the service of God".[29] For Radhakrishnan (the first edition of his annotated English translation was published in 1948), *dharmakṣetra* is the entire world, "the battleground for a moral struggle". Linked with this are the social and political dimensions of dharmic concern, now indicated as the "tasks and opportunities" of "religion".[30] Radhakrishnan's desire to present the message of the *Gītā* as universally applicable is clear in the array of terms with which he equates *dharma* in his commentary on 1.1.[31] In particular, he hints at an identity between the Hindu idea of the world as *karmabhūmi* and a Christian idea of the world as a vale of soul-making. It is worth bearing in mind that his concern to present to the western world an articulate philosophy of which Indians could be proud stemmed from an early experience at Madras Christian College. At that time, he was inclined to think that India's current lethargy might be due to its incoherent and world-denying philosophy, because of remarks made by A G Hogg about the *Gītā's* "ascetic and other-worldly tendencies" in his MA ethics classes.[32] Radhakrishnan's comment on 1.1 implicitly refutes such an interpretation of the *Gītā.*

For Tilak, involved in the struggle for Independence (though writing from jail in Mandalay, Burma, 1910-1911), the location of the *Gītā* is clear and crucial and indicates its central message. Using Mīmāṃsā criteria of exegesis, Tilak rejected any construction of the *Gītā* which relegates the battle to secondary status or prefers knowledge-as-renunciation over action.[33] It is true that his explanation of the *dharma*-field refers simply to a story from the *Mahābhārata*[34] and, like the rest of his massive commentary, makes no overt political reference. However, as Robert Stevenson argues, it is surely correct to read Tilak's interpretation of the *Gītā's* "Energism" as a way of motivating Hindus to political activity, along with his revival of a Ganesh festival and inauguration of another honouring the military leader, Shivaji.[35] There is probably a nationalist point in Tilak's comment that "the present city of Delhi stands on this field" (p.852).

For Prabhupāda, commenting in quite another context in the USA of the late 1960s,[36] the field is significant because it is the place where the Supreme Personality of Godhead "was present personally on this planet for the guidance of mankind" (p.2) and on which the unwanted, irreligious "plants" (sic, continuing the metaphor of the 'field' of *dharma)* were wiped out, so that "the thoroughly religious persons, headed by Yudhiṣṭhira, would be established by the Lord" (p.3). He indicates strongly that the *Gītā* should be read "with the help of a person who is a devotee of Śrī Krishna" and that one should "try to understand it without personally motivated interpretations" (p.1). Śaṃkara, 1300 years ago, would have agreed, though for him it was the teaching of non-duality which was given with the text through the correct teaching tradition *(sampradāya).*[37] I will return to the implications of these different views of what constitutes the field of *dharma* at the end.

What Gandhi, Radhakrishnan, Prabhupāda and many other neo-Hindu commentators share is a reinterpretation of *sva-dharma* and *varṇa-dharma.* In different ways, they all argue that *varṇa* is *not* to do with birth as such but with the kind of person one is (Radhakrishnan making much of Krishna's comment that he established the *varṇas* with respect to *guṇas* (qualities) and *karman* (actions) and making no mention of birth, p.160-1). This enables *dharma* to be universalised and *sva-dharma* to be variously related to an individual's own talents or abilities, though in the context of social responsibility. What is, at least in theory, left behind in such interpretations is the social and ritual system of caste much criticised in the encounter with the West. This system[38] is now distanced from the perceived textual ideal of a society upheld by people fulfilling different functions in accordance with their own gifts and preferences.[39] This does not, however, engender agreement on what the nature of such newly dharmic activity should be. For Gandhi it is *satyāgraha, ahiṃsā,* a Salt March, fasting. For Tilak it was violent participation in the nationalist struggle, if necessary recognising that what would be adharmic for others is *dharma* for the *sthitaprajña,* the person established in wisdom, for he (she?) has a different perspective.[40] For Prabhupāda, commenting from quite a different point of view, it is devotional service to the Lord in its many varieties.[41]

What, then, of the final moment? Though the Lord conducts the world according to fixed law and expects us to conform to the law of right actions based on our nature and station in life, explains Radhakrishnan, if we take shelter in Him we transcend all these (op.cit., p.378). As throughout the commentary, he glosses this in language which reaches across the divides of religious traditions, particularly to Christianity, speaking of "total self-giving to God", "the power of the spirit which changes every situation" (p.378). This, however, raises questions about the framework within which such transcended dharmic action is to be understood. Is this, in the end, the framework of some particular religious tradition (whether ISKCON, Advaita or some other), or is any religious path at all deemed of equal worth? And will Vivekananda's interpretation of the four yogas in the *Gītā* do as a model here?[42] What, then, of the atheist with a concern for *dharma,* whether modern-day inheritor of the Pūrva Mīmāṃsaka ritualists or a twentieth-century secularist?[43] This leads to our final reflections.

Questions Dharma raises

Our concluding reflections will, once again, be based on the three moments we have been considering, though the emphasis will be on the first, "on the field of *dharma,* Kurukṣetra". At the Conference I raised a series of questions, revolving around the issue of who has the right or, conversely, the duty to be on the field of *dharma* in an exploration of ethics for our time. I repeat them here, together with some further questions and comments made by participants in response. Taking my lead from the particular setting of the *Gītā,* I queried:

> "Should some of us survey the situation from afar with blind king, Dhṛtarāṣṭra, or even further afield? We do not belong to the Kuru clan. Or do we, if this is a universal story? In this case, do we in fact have any choice? As human beings, are we all necessarily on the field of *dharma,* deciding the nature of ethical action, torn by the struggles ourselves? But then is "ethical action or even intention" sufficiently particular to the *Gītā's* complex nuances of *dharma(s)* — the situation-and person-specific customs and duties; cosmic order intimately linked with yet transcending these (with Krishna as its ground and protector) — or but a simplistic reduction of these?"

Again:

> "If we choose to watch from afar, do we then have the right to interpret the nature of *dharma* ? Or, conversely, do we actually have a duty to do so, if we are not to slip into moral relativism? But if this is the case, what is the nature of the authority of the interpreter of *dharma*? That of a supposedly neutral western scholar? Or of one who has tried to live by *dharma* all their life — but in which tradition? Or is it only

that of Lord Krishna himself, so that our individual readings-in should be resisted? Or can we recognise that if the *Gītā* speaks to us at all it is to our own individual and corporate fields of quandaries?"

Further:

"Is the question of who has the right to interpret *dharma* just an issue for those of us sensitive to charges of Orientalism in Indological studies? Or what about dalits' rejection of Gandhi, refusing to be reincorporated into what they see as a system of *dharma* extended to all, which for generations had marginalised and oppressed them?[44] And can assertions of common cultural heritage be dangerous, when religious differences are either ignored or ignited?[45] This is *dharma* as concerned with intention, boundaries, power."

Finally:

"What of a view which seeks to extend religious and ethical understanding, not by positing some common *philosophia perennis,* as Radhakrishnan did, but by precisely recognising and trying not to subsume someone else's worldview into my own (as Krishna, of course, persistently does in the *Gītā*)?"

So I conclude by asking you: Whose world are we to uphold? On what basis? What part do the particularities of my own individual, social and religious situation have to play? And what can be the role of a gathering like this, in our pluralist and indeed communalist era, in deepening our understanding of *dharma,* of one another and of our world(s)?

Responses to these questions were numerous and shown in many ways. Here I intend simply to draw on a few of the contributions which were made on paper at the end of the discussion, for they seem to me to represent much that was said and, in particular, the spirit of engagement of many.

Interpretations of the "field of *dharma*" were numerous: the individual mind, contemporary British society, the conditions for interreligious dialogue — to name but a few. In the words of various participants:

"For me the battle of Kurukshetra is in me — right here. How to carry out my *dharma*? How can I uphold my traditions, culture and righteousness in this materialistic and divisive society?"[46]

"Battlefield: How to maintain and preserve my own traditions and values; to carry on and sustain values of life, and human values against material society and debased values. The field is right here and now in our own heart. We must try to preserve what we love and cherish."

"If the field is the individual's soul, how does it relate to what the Prophet Muhammad described as the Greater Jihad?"

"If we accept that we are all — regardless of creed/culture — on the field of *dharma*, then how can we practise the universals of *yama* and *niyama* [self-control and restraint] and at the same time respect cultural diversity? How can we be subject to the non-personal and also acknowledge personal, that is, individual value?"

"We're all on the battlefield. Isn't that notion a prerequisite of interreligious dialogue?"

Other comments concerned the notion of what is dharmic today, relating more to the second and third moments. For some respondents, Indian and non-Indian alike, the crucial issue was how westerners can come to understand the meaning of *dharma*. "What adjustments and translations need to be made in a western culture to begin to understand the concept of *dharma*?" Essays such as this may make some small contribution to this. However, it was clear that there were two much greater issues that participants wished to tackle. First, how those not brought up in a particular cultural tradition could start to understand the lived reality of *dharma* and, second, how those who were nurtured in such a tradition, but in a different context, could start to work out the implications of dharmic living in a society whose norms seemed very different.

Given this, it is appropriate to raise the issue of the status of women at this juncture. In his essay Dermot Killingley points out that the *Gītā* is almost shy in its treatment of the female, though it connects women's debauchery with the downfall of society in 1.41. Women are also included with Vaiśyas and Śūdras as examples of the lowest of the low who, nonetheless, are acceptable devotees to Krishna and can reach the highest goal (9.32). In his exploration of the *puruṣārthas*, Gavin Flood raises the possibility of deriving a pluralist and flexible model from them, a model which would allow for the reinterpretation of traditional attitudes to *strī-dharma*. For at least some female participants, this echoed their own perceptions. Commenting on this from the perspective of the three moments, we might suggest that the view of *dharma* with which Arjuna starts (including his nightmare of 1.41) has to be transcended in understanding the liberated equality of those who take refuge in Krishna, the truly dharmic state.

This is far from suggesting that the *Gītā* teaches social equality, whether of men and women or of Brahmins and Śūdras. It seems quite clear that it does not. In terms of the third moment, currently understood however, there does seem to be the possibility of at least three quite distinct readings. The first is to renounce attachment to the fruits of one's traditional gendered role, finding in that *dharma* (and refuge in Krishna?) the proper fulfillment of a *puruṣārtha.* This tunes with the growing recognition that the values of western feminism cannot be simply imported into Indian discussions of women's issues, a view held strongly, for example, by the editor of the journal, *Manushi.* The second is to renounce one particular way of reading *varṇāśrama-dharma,* in which marriage replaces for women other *saṃskāras* linked with the different stages of life. Three women offered reflections on "what *dharma* means to us as Hindu women", one explicitly in terms of the four stages of life, each of which she saw as applying to herself. Another acknowledged that *dharma* changes with each stage:

> "As a wife and mother, my *dharma* at present is towards my family, to look after them and to try to be there for their needs. However, with my later duty, my role also changes towards the community to relieve the sufferings of the needy. As I grow old and my duties are relinquished from the *gṛhastha* stage, my *dharma* will change again".

The third stated clearly:

> "*Dharma* for me is the *dharma* of the householder, the straightforward concerns of moral duty and obligations to myself, family and the society, thus acquiring wealth and success and pleasure and salvation".

Then quoting 1.1 in Sanskrit, she mused: "But then I think, is it destined or is it a choice I make?"

This leads to the third possibility. For a choice to accept such a view of *dharma* entails that there is a possibility of rejecting it too. For some the renunciation of all *dharmas* at this point may well include the rejection of traditional roles for women, the subjection to father, husband and sons advocated in the much-quoted verse from *Manu Smṛti* 9.3. It is not clear that this moves further from the *Gītā* than the caste-rejecting interpretations of *sva-dharma* mentioned above. If this is so, there seems no reason why gender should not be added to the list of community, nation, species, as a mundane division to be transcended,[47] though whether this is just by attitude towards it or through social reform as well will remain a matter for debate.

I conclude by returning to the first verse of the *Gītā*, whose initial words are actually: *dhṛtarāṣṭra uvāca:* Dhṛtarāṣṭra said. I suggest that they gently indicate a multi-faceted picture, seen, as subtle *dharma* is throughout the *Mahābhārata*, through different characters' eyes. In Krishna, eternal protector of everlasting *dharma*, a multiplicity of understandings may be united. But ours, perhaps, remains a kaleidoscopic picture compiled through Krishna's teaching, Arjuna's attempts to understand, Saṃjaya's vision granted by Vyāsa, Dhṛtarāṣṭra trying blindly to comprehend. Then there are the sages hearing the story again in a Brahminical hermitage, numerous commentators ancient and modern grappling with significance, the West watching Peter Brook's version and listening to the critics who accuse him of evacuating the *Gītā's* meaning in reducing it to an *unoverheard* conversation. This suggests that there is no simplistic way of applying the *Gītā's* teaching on *dharma* to the multiple questions which face us in upholding our world. But a new conversation has been started. In the sounding silence so eloquently expressed by Nicholas Lash in his essay, may we hear.

1 My thanks go to the audience at the Inaugural Conference who shaped this paper in many ways, not least by their willingness to raise and discuss questions amongst themselves.
2 See J Lipner, 1994: ch.8, esp.p.218.
3 "With Chapter III the *Gita* ends. It need not have been followed by anything more.....The rest of the *Gita* is intended to explain more clearly what has been said in the first three chapters"; M.K. Gandhi, n.d: 303
4 That is, "an inquiry into the ethics of the *Bhagavadgītā* for *our* times", with a mixed, general audience in mind.
5 "For the Hindu [the *Gītā*] is now the *one book* of books.....The Gita is as fresh as ever and just as to the Christian is the Bible [sic].....the Gita is to the Hindu": Rai Bahadur Lala Baijnath (1908) as quoted in R Minor (ed.), 1986: 4.
6 Cf Sheldon Pollock's argument that the medieval *nibandhas* on *dharma* are "a fertile source for understanding the variety of inequality constructions" of that time, involving "not just the instrumental use of knowledge (indeed, of *veda)* in the essentialization and dichotomization of the social order, but the very control of knowledge.....", in C A Breckenridge and P van der Veer (eds.), 1993: 104-5.
7 See, for example, the continuing debates about the nature of the study of religion(s) as distinct from theology reflected in the recent journal, *Method and Theory in the Study of Religion,* and the editors' refusal to publish articles which they see as being written from a theological perspective.
8 "This is not 'Peter Brook's *Mahabharata*'; this is the Indian epic *Mahabharata,* lovingly recast by Brook into a form which non-Indian audiences can share": John Smith, writing in the *Times Literary Supplement,* quoted in Garry O'Connor, 1989: 61.
9 E.g., articles by Gautam Dasgupta and Rustom Bharucha in David Williams (ed.), 1991.
10 See 18.66, which Rāmānuja's school takes as the *caramaśloka* or culminating verse of the text.
11 Supported, though not explicitly argued, by the case Robert Minor makes in his article, 1980: 339-54.
12 There is a plausible argument which suggests that either the *Gītā* is to be read as a separate text or it is to be taken as integral to the *Mahābhārata,* but that the two approaches are incompatible (see J Brockington's essay). However, when we are reflecting on its significance now, it is clear that both these positions have been taken in the tradition (separate readings by Vedānta commentators, heard as an episode of the *Mahābhārata* in many Hindus' reception of its teaching). It seems appropriate to benefit from the richness of resonances which may be thus derived.
13 Halbfass, 1988: esp. ch.17.
14 The exceptions are the Buddhists, but they belong to an Indian universe of discourse all the same.
15 In fact, given a reading which sees *dharma* as fundamental to a Brahminical view of the universe, we should not be surprised if it is not crucial to the worldview of many Hindus at all.
16 See Sheldon Pollock, op.cit., note 6.
17 In *Mahābhārata* terms, this is the battle effecting the transition between the Dvāpara and Kali Yugas. It thus re-establishes an admittedly more fragile cosmic and social order after a liminal period of chaos. The battle is also a metaphor for the Kali Yuga itself (Lynn Thomas, "The Personification of Kali in the *Mahābhārata*", paper given at the Spalding Symposium for Indian Religions, Oxford, 1995).
18 *dharmasya tadbuddheś ca kṣetram abhivṛddhikāraṇaṃ yad tad ucyate kurukṣetram iti;* See G S Sadhale, 1935: 1.
19 M Biardeau, 1989: 42-3.
20 Despite modern readings, there seems no reason to doubt that *varṇa is* a matter of birth in the *Gītā.* 18.41f. clearly states that appropriate actions for each of the four *varṇas* are due to the (distribution of the three) *guṇas* deriving from their *svabhāva* (own nature). This is not abrogated by 4.13, where Krishna constructs the *varṇa* system according to *guṇas* (here probably qualities in general) and actions and birth are not mentioned. It is surely assumed that birth in a particular *varṇa* is the result of such qualities and actions.
21 See G Flood's essay.
22 W Sargeant's breakup of 8.3, giving this role to the *adhyātma* does not seem to me to be justified.
23 *yayedaṃ dhāryate jagat; etadyonīni bhūtāni sarvāṇīty upadhāraya, ahaṃ kṛtsnasya jagataḥ prabhavaḥ pralayas tathā.....mayi sarvam idaṃ protaṃ sūtre maṇigaṇā iva.*
24 All the translators I have consulted translate this as if it is a past event for which Krishna was responsible, e.g. Radhakrishnan: "The fourfold order was created by Me.....". However, the past participle here can equally be construed in the present: "The system of the four social groups is created by Me in proportion to qualities/constituents and actions" *(cāturvarṇyaṃ mayā sṛṣṭaṃ guṇakarmavibhāgaśaḥ).* This makes better sense of the connection between this and the previous verse and the following one in which Krishna speaks, in the *present* tense, saying, "Actions *do not* defile me" *(na māṃ karmāṇi limpanti).*
25 Halbfass' translation of *ātmatuṣṭi;* W Halbfass, 1988: 324. Halbfass notes that the *Mahābhārata* tends to mention only three sources: *veda, smṛti, śiṣṭācīrṇa,* op.cit., p.552, n.64.
26 *pattraṃ puṣpaṃ phalaṃ toyaṃ yo me bhaktyā prayacchati, tad ahaṃ bhaktyupahṛtam aśnāmi prayatātamanaḥ.*

27 This verse is the occasion for an extremely long comment defending his view against Mīmāṃsaka and *karmajñānasamuccaya* views.

28 *karmayogajñānayogabhaktiyogarūpān sarvān dharmān paramaniḥśreyasasādhanabhūtān madārādhanatvena atimātraprītyā yathādhikāraṃ kurvāṇa evoktarītya phalasaṅgakartṛtvādiparityāgena parityajya.....*

29 M K Gandhi, n.d.: 16. He also gives two further meanings, viz. that, "for a Kshatriya a battlefield is always a field of dharma", and that, where the Pandavas were present "could not be altogether a place of sin" (ibid.). Gandhi is sometimes accused of idiosyncratic allegorisation here. However, allegorisation of the *Mahābhārata* had already been used in the nineteenth century and the Theosophists, who affected his understanding, also allegorised. See R W Neufeldt, in R Minor, op.cit., ch.1.

30 S Radhakrishnan, 1949: 79-80. We cannot here discuss the modern use of *dharma* to mean "religion" except to note that it is anachronistic to read this back into the *Gītā.*

31 These equations include righteousness, what is right, knowledge of right and wrong (by implication), moral struggle, the path to "heaven", the making of saints, practice, religion, what promotes worldly prosperity, and spiritual freedom (the last following Śaṃkara).

32 S Gopal, 1989: 16.

33 B G Tilak, 1980: 37.

34 Kuru, the common ancestor of Kauravas and Pāṇḍavas, was ploughing the ground (hence, field) and was promised by Indra that anyone who dies there in war or performing austerities would obtain heaven (hence, *dharmakṣetra* or "sacred ground"); B G Tilak, op.cit., p.852.

35 See R N Minor (ed.), 1986: ch.3.

36 See A C Bhaktivedanta Swami Prabhupada, 1978 (reprint of the 1968 first edition).

37 See especially his Introduction to the *Gītābhāṣya* and his comment on 13.13.

38 Whether there is such a thing as "the caste system" and what place reactions to the West had in forming some modern manifestations of it is not the issue here.

39 Radhakrishnan, 1949, p.160-1: "The varṇa or the order to which we belong is independent of sex, birth or breeding. A class determined by temperament and vocation is not a caste determined by birth and heredity.....Today [the fourfold order] cannot be regarded as anything more than an insistence on a variety of ways in which the social purpose can be carried out.....The present morbid condition of India broken into castes and subcastes is opposed to the unity taught by the *Gītā,* which stands for an organic as against an atomistic conception of society".

Prabhupāda says, "In India, the *varṇāśrama* system has now been taken in a perverted way, and thus a man born in the family of a *brāhmaṇa*.....claims that he should be accepted as a *brāhmaṇa.* But this claim is not accepted by the *śāstra* (scripture).....Real *varṇāśrama-dharma* is based on the factual *quality* one has attained, regardless of birth or heredity"; A C Bhaktivedanta Swami, 1977: 118; see also 214.

Gandhi, in his talks on the *Gītā,* is rather more conservative than Radhakrishnan or Prabhupāda. While he asks about the *character* of the Brahmin and others and rejects the view that anyone is higher or lower than another, it would seem that "the person who cleans lavatories" (p.124) is nonetheless one born to this job. However, his ideas on *varṇāśrama-dharma* changed, particularly with the idea of each becoming a Śūdra (see M Chatterjee, 1983: 3). Judith Brown notes the influence of the Jain poet, Raychandbhai, in forming Gandhi's view of *dharma* as illumination from within, rather than as externally prescribed duties; J Brown, 1989: 77.

For Tilak, the arrangement of the four classes in accordance with different "inherently natural qualities" (op.cit., p.1195 on 18.41) is intended to ensure that "the various activities of the world should go on in an orderly way" (p.1194 on 18.40). The *varṇāśrama* system thus underpins his view that action is incumbent on everyone (cf.p.718, Appendix on relation of *Gītā* to *Mahābhārata*).

40 Cf R W Stevenson in R Minor (ed.), op.cit., p.57-60.

41 See his comment on 4.15b, translated "Therefore, as did the ancients, you should perform your duty in this divine consciousness": "To retire from activities and to sit aloof, making a show of Kṛṣṇa consciousness, is less important than actually engaging in the field of activities for the sake of Kṛṣṇa" (p.78).

42 Found throughout his *Complete Works;* see, e.g., vol.7, p.198.

43 Cf Prem Nath Bazaz, 1975. Bazaz sees the Brahminical and theistic teaching of the *Gītā* as one aspect of a dangerous ideology which has smothered other rationalist materialist strands of the Indian cultural heritage (see especially ch.42).

44 See J Lipner, 1994: 122, for a brief discussion of this criticism of Gandhi; see also E Zelliot, 1992.

45 Note the following comment from a Vishwa Hindu Parishad pamphlet circulating in Leicester in 1993, much of whose contents was considerably more inflammatory than the following: "Only Hindu unity can pave the way for Hindu, Muslim, Sikh, Dalit, Christian unity, national integration, prosperity and also Pakistan friendship. Hindu unity will come through Ram Mandir

construction in Ayodhya. It will bring good luck to India. It's a second movement for India's freedom. It will destroy Deshdrohi Ravanas [viz. demons hostile to India].....''; A Shankar (n.d.), *Warning: India in danger.* His comment that "many of the Muslims in India tend to support Pakistan. Whenever a Pakistani team wins a cricket match, they cry 'Pakistan Zindabad'" has disturbing resonances with Norman Tebbit, a former British Government minister's, infamous remark concerning British coloured immigrants' support of visiting cricket teams from their countries of origin. Issues of pluralism face us all.

46 Dr Sushil Soni. Other comments were unnamed.

47 See A C Bhaktivedanta Swami Prabhupada, 1978: 78.

Enjoying the World: Desire (kāma) & the Bhagavadgītā

Dermot Killingley

Desire in the Bhagavadgītā

The *Bhagavadgītā* abounds in words for desire, pleasure, enjoyment, wish, will, attachment, longing, and love.[1] Some of these words, such as *lobha* ("greed"), have moral connotations, but most of them are morally neutral. Passages referring to the opposite of desire — hatred or disgust — are also relevant; so are those on equanimity or indifference *(samatva, sāmya).* This is one of the recurrent topics of the poem. The yogi is characterised by an equal attitude to pleasure and pain (2.38, 6.32, 12.18), and to things that other people would consider desirable and undesirable: cows and dogs, or gold and clods or stones (5.18, 6.8).

The topic of desire is prominent not only in the teachings given by Krishna to Arjuna, but in the narrative frame of the poem. Arjuna's dilemma, which is the starting-point of this frame, is expressed in terms of desire. On the one hand, Arjuna desires power (1.33, 1.45), and so do his opponents (2.5c), and on the other hand, he does not desire enjoyments, victory or life itself if they are achieved at the cost of killing his kinsmen and elders (1.32, 2.5-8). Much of Krishna's teaching concerns the ideal of action without desire for fruit. It was this ideal, referred to as *niṣkāma-karma,* "desireless action" (a phrase which does not occur in the *Gītā,* but which sums up an important part of its teaching), that was emphasised when the *Gītā* became popular in

Bengal in the early twentieth century. But in the early part of his attempt to persuade Arjuna to fight, where Krishna uses more obvious arguments, he holds out the prospect of pleasure in heaven or on earth (2.32, 2.37), showing that he regards the pursuit of pleasure as legitimate for a member of the princely class. There is some tension between this view and the ideal of indifference to pain and pleasure which Krishna advocates for the yogi. The two are sharply juxtaposed in 2.37 and 2.38. Here, Krishna first tells Arjuna to fight because he will either gain heaven through death in battle or enjoy the earth through victory, and immediately afterwards tells him to fight without counting the difference between gain and loss or victory and defeat.

This juxtaposition occurs at a turning-point in the poem, where Krishna moves from arguments appealing to Arjuna's sense of heroism to the discussion of yoga. But the appeal to heroism is not abandoned; it reappears in a more sophisticated form, using the terminology of the three *guṇas*. Arjuna is urged to carry out his innate action *(svabhāvajaṃ karma),* in accordance with his *guṇa*-disposition. In the traditional allocation of *guṇas* to the *varṇas* (which the *Gītā* summarises (18.41) though does not spell out), the Kṣatriya is dominated by *rajas,* often translated "passion", which is characterised by the active pursuit of desires.[2] By pursuing legitimate pleasure, therefore, Arjuna would be following his own *dharma;* his attempt to avoid this pursuit is contrary to his own *dharma,* and therefore fraught with danger (3.35).

The Silence of the Bhagavadgītā on Sexual Desire

Since the *Gītā* says so much about desire and pleasure, it is remarkable that it says almost nothing about what elsewhere is often referred to simply as *kāma, par excellence:* sexual desire and pleasure. This is a common enough topic in other Sanskrit literature, including the *Mahābhārata* as a whole and the Upaniṣads. The faculty of reproduction is regularly listed as one of the five faculties of action in Sāṃkhya texts, and in the older lists of faculties to be found in the Brāhmaṇas and Upaniṣads. It is true that the *Bhagavadgītā* mentions the ten plus one faculties *(indriya)* of a person (11.5), which is a clear reference to the standard Sāṃkhya list of eleven faculties which includes the faculty of reproduction. But these are never fully enumerated in the *Gītā,* and when a list of activities is given (5.8-9), the reproductive faculty is not mentioned, although the other four faculties of action are (speaking, grasping, walking and defecating), as well as the five sense faculties: hearing, touch, sight, taste (represented here by eating) and smell. There is a brief hint about the sexual desires of women, which are liable to lead to mixture of castes when the *dharma* of a family is destroyed (1.41), but the poem is mostly about men, and their sexual desires are not mentioned even in passages on the power and danger of desire. It is desire for food *(rasa)* that is mentioned as the last to leave the yogi (2.59), and it is in terms of desire for food that Arjuna expresses his longing for Krishna's teaching (10.18). The representation of God as the male lover and the devotee as the female lover, which is the basis of so much of the literature and theology of *bhakti,* is briefly touched on once by Arjuna, but in a mere two words (11.44d). Even when sexual imagery is used for God's creative activity (14.3), the womb in which God places the seed is identified not with the feminine noun *prakṛti* which is used elsewhere in the *Gītā,* but with the neuter *brahman,* so that the sexuality of the image is suppressed.

This absence of sex even where it is expected may be insipid to modern taste. When we examine it further, we may even find it offensive. The one passage which mentions sexual desire, as we saw, is about the sexual desires of women (1.41), a familiar theme in Dharma literature and in tales, where women's sexuality is seen as a snare and a source of danger, leading to chaos if it is not controlled. The frequency of this theme reflects a male outlook which identifies sexual desire with the other — that which has to be controlled — the female. Elsewhere in the *Gītā* the female is avoided, just as sex is. In ch. 10, where Krishna identifies himself with manifestations of his glory *(vibhūti),* we might expect his feminine manifestations *(nārī)* to include glorious examples of submissive womanhood such as Arundhatī or Sītā, if not a more forceful woman such as Draupadī. But instead, he gives a list of grammatically feminine nouns: *kīrti,* "fame"; *śrī,* "glory"; *vāc,* "speech"; *smṛti,* "memory"; *dhṛti,* "steadfastness"; *kṣamā,* "patience". These are not names of organically female beings (except possibly *śrī* and *vāc,* which are goddesses), but abstractions. When Arjuna speaks of his former social relations with Krishna, apologising for treating him familiarly without realising that he was God (11.41-2), he evokes a blokish matiness that is associated today with insecurity in relation to women, or with downright misogyny.

This sexist aspect of the *Bhagavadgītā* is not its most pleasant side or its most interesting. Few commentators have remarked on it, if any. It is, as I have suggested, offensive to modern minds. I have dwelt on it because I want to point out that when we use an ancient text as a source of ideas for the modern world, we have to be selective. As Rāmānuja says of the Veda, we take what we need and leave the rest, just as we take only what we need from a well full of water.[3]

The Ideal of Desirelessness

Perhaps the most frequent occurrence of desire in the *Bhagavadgītā* is in the form of something to avoid. For this reason, many of the terms for desire which we have noted occur with a negative prefix *niḥ-* or *a-*. The yogi, whom Krishna presents as the ideal person, abandons desires (2.55; 2.71). Desire, arising from attachment *(saṅga)* is part of a train of faults which lead to destruction (2.62f). The pursuit of enjoyment in heaven, even through ritual activity enjoined by the Veda, is condemned (2.43-5). The reason why desire is to be avoided is that action without desire is the way out of the bondage of action which leads to rebirth. It is impossible to avoid action itself (3.5-6), but by avoiding desire we can act in a way that does not lead to bondage. In the thought-world of the *Bhagavadgītā,* bondage — the bondage of karma and rebirth — is closely associated with action.[4] Any action which does not lead to bondage can therefore be paradoxically called actionlessness (4.18). It can also be called both *saṃnyāsa* and *yoga* (6.1).[5] The view that bondage is caused by desire, rather than by action itself, is prominent in Buddhism (as John Brockington mentions in his essay). But it also appears already in *Bṛhadāraṇyaka Upaniṣad* 4.4.5-7, where, after one of the earliest statements of the doctrine of rebirth according to action, it is pointed out that action is determined by resolve *(kratu),* which in turn is determined by desire, and one who is free from desire is not reborn but goes to *brahman.*

Legitimation of Desire

As we have seen in connection with Krishna's appeal to Arjuna's *dharma* as a Kṣatriya, the *Bhagavadgītā* also presents a positive aspect to desire which contrasts with this ideal of desirelessness. God himself is desire, such as does not conflict with *dharma* (7.11).There is in fact a close relationship between the concepts of desire and *dharma*, which can be shown from other literature. First of all, these two aims are grouped with *artha* (wealth and power) in the well-known triad of worldly aims discussed in Gavin Flood's essay. Further, there are three areas in which the satisfaction of desires is a legitimate aim: householdership, kingship, and sacrifice (these areas can overlap, since the same man can be householder, king and patron of the sacrifice or *yajamāna*).The householder, in contrast to men in the other three stages of life, is entitled to pursue pleasures, including sexual pleasure. The king has the triple function of enjoying, upholding and protecting the earth. His relationship to the earth is thus analogous to the householder's relationship to his wife, or rather, it is a special case of it, since the earth *(bhūmi*, feminine noun) is the wife, or one of the wives, of the king, just as the earth, supported by Viṣṇu in his boar-*avatāra*, is a wife of Viṣṇu who is the prototype of the king. Thirdly, a sacrifice is performed in order to gain a reward such as long life, the birth of a son, or a secure place in the worlds beyond death. Desire is thus the motive of ritual action, and of righteous action in general (Manu 2.2-5; cf. the *Īśa Upaniṣad*, 1-2).

The link between desire and ritual action is provided by the concept of *saṃkalpa*, which is both the intention or determination to perform a ritual and the expectation of a specific reward as a result of it. *Saṃkalpa* is an essential element in Vedic ritual, and any vows or rules of restraint one may undertake result from *saṃkalpa* also (Manu 2.3). The *Bhagavadgītā* makes explicit references to Vedic ritual, and the ritualistic theory of *saṃkalpa* can help us to understand it. *Gītā* 3.9 tells us that sacrifice is the one kind of action that does not bind. If it is indeed desire and not action that causes bondage, we might suppose that sacrifice does not bind because it is free from desire. But sacrifice can hardly be free from desire, since *saṃkalpa* is necessary to it. Indeed, the next verse (3.10) calls sacrifice the mythical cow which grants all desires. The following verses explain that through sacrifice we give back to the universe, or to the gods, what we have taken for our enjoyment. This is expressed in terms of food and the payment of debts: if we eat without performing sacrifice, we are thieves (3.12). The bondage of action is thus seen as a form of debt, incurred through the act of eating, which is annulled if it is repaid through sacrifice. Bondage is to be escaped not by not acting, nor yet by not desiring, but by satisfying our desires exclusively through that transaction between the worldly and the divine which is called sacrifice. The distinctive feature of this kind of action, which marks it as free from bondage, is not the absence of desire but the presence of a motive which lies outside the person who acts.

Though the *Gītā* uses the terminology of Vedic ritual, the term "sacrifice" has to be understood in a wider sense. All our actions, and not merely ritual actions, can be performed as offerings to God: "Whatever you do, whatever you eat, whatever you offer in sacrifice, and whatever you give, do it as a gift to me" (9.27). By performing our actions in this way we are freed from bondage (9.28). Ritual theory classifies actions as periodical *(nitya),* occasional *(naimittika),* and optional *(kāmya).* It is the last, as their name implies, which are directly based on desire, since they are only performed by people who desire fruits from them. The *Gītā* does not use this classification explicitly,[6] though it is used by Rāmānuja.[7]

Desirelessness and Motivation

Manu says that nothing in this world is free from desire: the study of the Veda, and the ritual activity which the Veda enjoins, are results of desire (Manu, 2.2). If this is so, then even what is done for God is done from a desire to please him or to do his will. The yogi who is devoted to God and has God as his highest concern *(mad-bhakto mat-parāyanaḥ, Gītā* 9.34) could even be said to desire God. Even the gods long for the vision of God's universal form *(darśana-kāṅkṣiṇaḥ,* 11.52), and Krishna's teaching makes Arjuna long to hear more: he cannot be satiated with its nectar *(tṛptir hi śṛṇvato nāsti me'mṛtam,* 10.18). Similarly "salvation" or liberation could be called an object of desire; so how can there ever be desirelessness? The *Bhagavadgītā* expresses this problem in terms of the three strands or qualities *(guṇa)* of nature: all three cause bondage, and though the highest of them, *sattva* ("goodness"), is stainless, illuminating and free from disease, and is repeatedly contrasted with the second *guṇa, rajas* ("passion"), as leading to disinterested action, it binds by attachment to bliss and knowledge (14.6). To unravel the *Gītā's* teaching on desire further, we must look at its teaching on the *guṇas*.

The *guṇas* are thought of in the *Gītā* mainly in terms of their influence on a person's character and behaviour. In the lists of the examples of the effects of each of the *guṇa*s on a person in chapters 14, 17 and 18, a clear pattern emerges. If *sattva* predominates in a person's character, that person seeks and finds long-term satisfaction, even at the expense of short-term privation. The person dominated by *rajas* seeks and finds short-term satisfaction, and the person dominated by the third *guṇa, tamas* ("darkness"), is so lazy and stupid that he gets no satisfaction at all. The pattern is clear in the matter of food. The sāttvik person likes healthy, strengthening food which promotes happiness and satisfaction; the rājasik person likes strongly flavoured food which causes pain, misery and sickness, and the tāmasik person likes rotten food that has lost its taste and is past its sell-by date *(paryuṣita;* 17.8-10). In general, *sattva* leads to long-term happiness that begins like poison and ends like nectar, *rajas* leads to short-term happiness that begins like nectar and ends like poison, and *tamas* leads to a happiness that is illusory in both the short and the long term, being merely the result of sleep, idleness and negligence (18.37-9).

So far, the *guṇa* theory seems to point to no more than an intelligent, far-seeing self-interest. But some passages about the *guṇa*s go further. For instance, while the rājasik person gives with the expectation of favours in return, the sāttvik person gives because it is right to give *(dātavyam iti,* 17.20-21). Similarly, while the rājasik person performs worship with a view to its rewards or fruits, the sāttvik person worships because it is right to worship *(yaṣṭavyam iti,* 17.11). The *Gītā* thus rejects Manu's view that all action is motivated by desire. Rather, it holds that the highest form of action is motivated outside the agent, in the categorical imperatives of *dharma.*

WORSHIP

The topic of worship or sacrifice *(yajña)* brings us back to *Gītā* 3.9, where it is said that sacrifice is the only kind of action that is not binding. As we saw, this can be read together with *Gītā* 9.27-8, where we are told that all our actions can be done as offerings to God, and thereby do not cause bondage. The *Bhagavadgītā* solves the problem of the bondage of action through what has been called a Copernican reversal: instead of seeing ourselves as the centre of our action, as pre-Copernican astronomy saw the earth as the centre of the universe, we are asked to see God as the centre of our actions, as Copernicus saw the sun as the centre.[8] In this way action is cast off *(saṃ-ny-as)* on to God (3.30; 18.57), so that one can be a renouncer *(saṃnyāsin)* while still acting. The concept of God, and the associated concept of worship, allow us to think of action which is motivated outside the agent. Merely to be indifferent to success or failure, happiness or unhappiness, does not solve the problem of the bondage of action, because if taken to the extreme it leaves us with no motive at all. The *Gītā's* solution is that we should act not for ourselves but for God, making our actions acts of worship. We can thus further God's aims: the welfare of the world, and our own salvation.

For even God, who is the exemplar of the yogi, does not act in a totally unmotivated way. He does not act to fulfil any needs of his own, since he has none (3.22). Yet he continues in action as an example to others (3.23f), and the yogi should do the same, both to avoid confusing others (3.26), and for the maintenance of the world (3.20, 25). Besides maintaining the world in being (10.42), God acts in two specific ways: he takes birth in the world in order to rescue the righteous, destroy evildoers and establish *dharma* (4.8), and he returns the love of his devotees (12.14-20). In Arjuna's case, Krishna returns his love by instructing him (10.1), by showing him his universal form (11.54), and finally by promising that Arjuna will reach God (18.65). In loving his devotees, God breaks his own rule of holding no one either hateful or dear (9.29; cf.9.4f). In this too he is the exemplar of the yogi, who has no desires (5.3; 12.17), yet is devoted to God.

Near the end of his teaching, Krishna tells Arjuna: "Do as you wish" *(yathecchasi tathā kuru,* 18.63). This is surprising in view of Arjuna's original wish not to fight, but the preceding verses show that Krishna intends Arjuna not merely to fight, which he is going to do anyway because all beings are controlled by God (18.59-61), but to fight willingly. This throws light on Krishna's earlier statement that action is far inferior to discipline of mental attitude *(buddhi-yoga,* 2.49). Arjuna misunderstands this statement, taking it to mean that action is inferior to inaction (3.1),[9] but we can understand it as meaning that it is not what you do that determines whether you are reborn, and if so in what form, but the motivation that causes you to do it and the way you understand the relation between your action and yourself (cf.9.30: *samyag-vyavasita).*

The Bhagavadgītā for Today

The *Bhagavadgītā* has been interpreted by Indian commentators according to the concerns of their respective theological schools. In modern times, it has been interpreted by Indians and others from various points of view. When it became popular among Indian nationalists in the early twentieth century, the ideal of action without desire for fruit was emphasised, and commentators from Gandhi onwards have found social or spiritual programmes in the *Gītā.* This should not be taken to imply that the text itself is meaningless; rather, the variety of interpretations is evidence of its vitality. What can we learn today from the *Bhagavadgītā,* particularly about desire and enjoyment?

First, we can learn a norm of action which is not based on the satisfaction of our immediate desires. The classification of the three *guṇas* is helpful here, since it points to an ideal of sāttvik action which is based on *dharma,* and which enables us to enjoy the world in the long term. Next, we can look again at the *Gītā's* view of worship as a repayment for what we enjoy. If we apply this idea to our modern concern with the environment, we can understand one side of the transaction: we can see that we consume enormous quantities, not only of food but of fuel and materials, and produce similar quantities of useless or dangerous waste. But what of the other side of this transaction: how can we repay the debt we incur by consuming? We are unlikely to be satisfied with the idea that we can repay what we take from the environment by performing Vedic sacrifices, even of the more environment-friendly kinds which do not involve slaughter of animals or burning huge quantities of firewood.[10] Even a simple offering of a leaf, a flower, a fruit or water (9.26) may seem irrelevant to the problem. But the *Gītā's* view of worship is not limited to rituals, even of this elementary kind. In the same verse we are told that God accepts the offering from the giver who gives his (or her)[11] own self. It is the giving of oneself that is crucial, not the material offering. Then follows the verse we have quoted before: everything we do can be made an offering to God (9.27), and thereby we are freed from the bondage of action (9.28). To give ourselves to God and to make our actions an offering to him is to further his purpose, which, as we have seen, includes the maintenance of the world and the establishment of *dharma.* Accordingly, the yogi's action has for its purpose the maintenance of the world (3.20, 3.25).

The *Bhagavadgītā* also speaks of knowledge as freedom from the bondage of action: it is the fire which reduces all action to ashes (4.37; cf.4.19). Here too, reference is made to Vedic ritual: the worship which consists of knowledge is better than any material offering (4.33), and knowledge is associated with absence of attachment and the performance of actions for the purpose of worship alone (4.23). This form of knowledge is referred to as *buddhi-yoga,* "discipline of mental attitude" (2.49, 10.10, 18.57).[12] It involves not just knowledge of how the universe and ourselves are constituted, but an attitude of detachment in relation to both.

In the *Gītā's* metaphysics, our bodies and minds are not ourselves, nor are they something we own. This contrasts with a common modern attitude which treats our bodies as if we owned, maintained and used them like a car. We have come to think of our bodies as instruments through which we can have pleasure, or through which we can earn money to buy pleasures. We tend to treat our minds as instruments in the same way — as if they were computers. We talk about them in terms of information-input and programming. But our bodies and minds are not like cars or computers. For one thing, we cannot switch them off and walk away. As Rāmānuja saw, we and our bodies are *a-pṛthak-siddha:* that is, we cannot conceivably exist without them, or they without us. For another thing, our bodies are continuous with the environment from which we draw air, food and water, and into which we exhale, excrete and sweat. Our bodies are part of nature *(prakṛti).* So, too, are our minds, which are shaped by our material and social environment through perception and language.

Nature, the *Bhagavadgītā* tells us, belongs to God (7.4). Those who think otherwise are described in ch.16, which refers to such people as demonic *(āsura).* This chapter stands out from the rest of the poem as much as ch.11, though in a different way. While most of the poem is about the ideal person, the yogi, who at his best is devoted to God and dear to God (12.14-20), ch.16 is about the opposite kind of person. Historically, we may read it as an attack on the ancient Indian materialist school, the Lokāyatas or Cārvākas; but we can also read it as an attack on present-day materialists. Instead of saying that the world belongs to God and is supported and overseen by him (7.5-7, 9.4, 9.8, 9.10), they say it is driven by desire. Instead of seeing God as the centre of their world, they see themselves as the centre. They are the embodiment of *ahaṃkāra,* which in the *Gītā* is both a metaphysical concept, the part of nature which is manifested in our capacity to see ourselves as "I", and also a moral concept, selfishness. The demonic man[13] thinks in terms of himself. His attitude is expressed in 16.13f: "I have won this object of desire, I am going to win that, I have got this wealth, and I am going to have that.....I am successful, I am strong, I am happy, I will worship,[14] I will make gifts, I will have fun".

In modern times, the demonic person is less likely to worship, but he or she may still say, "I've discovered the religion that suits me", as well as saying, "I've got a right to be happy in my own way, I've got my own life to lead, I can use my credit card". Such people are misled by false knowledge *(ajñānavimohitāḥ,* 16.15). They are brought to hell by desire, anger and greed, but by avoiding these three essentially self-centred attitudes we can reach the highest (16.22).

Desire, anger and greed are described in this passage as the triple gate of hell which destroys the self (16.21). This recalls a closely related text, the *Īśā Upaniṣad,* which says that those who destroy themselves, or destroy the Self, enter demonic worlds that are covered in blind darkness (Īśā Up., 3). There has been much discussion of what it is that such people are said to destroy. The word used, *ātman,* has both an everyday meaning, "themselves", and a technical meaning, "the underlying essence of a person".[15] In the present context, we can understand the verse as meaning that by seeing ourselves as the centre of the universe, and therefore seeing the satisfaction of our desires as the ultimate goal, we have a false view of ourselves, and therefore are unable to find true fulfillment. Returning to the passage in the *Gītā,* we are told that if we take this view — and it is a commonly held view today — we hate God in our own bodies and in those of others (16.18), because in seeking our own satisfaction we deny that of others, and oppose God's aim which is the maintenance of the world.

Much of what the *Bhagavadgītā* says is summed up in the first verse of the *Īśā Upaniṣad:*

Īśāvāsyam idaṃ sarvaṃ yat kiṃ ca jagatyāṃ jagat
tena tyaktena bhuñjītha mā gṛdhaḥ kasya svid dhanam

The verse is very condensed and ambiguous, but it seems to tell us that the world is to be worn by God; that is to say, its purpose is to be his clothing. We should enjoy it by renouncing it. We can understand this renunciation in the sense we have learnt from the *Gītā:* to renounce the world is to acknowledge that it belongs to God and not to ourselves, and to act in it without attachment (18.9). The Upaniṣad adds that we are not to covet anyone's wealth, for covetousness is a particularly perverted form of desire, which is centred not only on oneself but on what does not in any sense belong to oneself.

The true way to enjoy the world, according to these two texts, is to take from it what we need, but to repay it in worship of God, which takes the form of action which shares in God's concern for the world. Such action is to be performed in the knowledge that no part of the world, not even our own minds and bodies, belongs to ourselves, but only to God.

1 Expressions in this semantic area include the nouns *kāma, sukha, bhoga, icchā, āśiṣ, saṃkalpa, saṅga, rajas, rāga, anuṣvaṅga* (13.9), the verbs *icchati, kāṅkṣati, bhuṅkte,* and also the desiderative forms of verbs, compounds ending in *-artha* meaning "having as one's aim", or *-para* meaning "concerned with, intent on", and the use of the dative case to express purpose.
2 According to Śaṃkara's commentary on *Gītā* 18.41, the Brahmin is characterised by *sattva,* the Kṣatriya primarily by *rajas* and secondarily by *sattva,* the Vaiśya primarily by *rajas* and secondarily by *tamas,* and the Śūdra primarily by *tamas* and secondarily by *rajas.* Etymologically, *rajas* is connected with *rāga,* "attachment".
3 J A B van Buitenen, 1968: 61.
4 *Karmaṇā badhyate jantur vidyayā tu pramucyate; tasmāt karma na kurvanti yatayaḥ pāradarśinaḥ:* "By action a person is bound, by knowledge a person is freed. Therefore, sages who have perfect vision do not perform actions". Mbh., *Mokṣadharma,* 12.233.7.
5 *Saṃnyāsa,* literally "throwing down, casting off", is the renunciation of all ritual actions, as well as all actions that have social and economic significance, in pursuit of liberation. The renouncer *(saṃnyāsin)* performs no rituals and lives apart from society. *Saṃnyāsa* is the practical outcome of the view that action, which in Vedic contexts often refers to ritual action, is binding. The ideas underlying *saṃnyāsa* are admirably explained in P. Olivelle, 1992: 19-81. Through the notion that action need not be binding, the *Gītā* reinterprets *saṃnyāsa* in a way which makes it compatible with action in the world.
6 However, an implicit reference to this threefold classification may be found in 18.2, which defines renunciation *(saṃnyāsa)* as the giving up of desire-based *(kāmya)* actions.
7 See Rāmānuja's *Gītā-bhāsya,* 18.7; 18.9; J A B van Buitenen, 1968: pp.163f.
8 R V De Smet, 1977: 53-64.
9 There is no direct indication that Arjuna's question in 3.1 refers to 2.49, but there is no other verse to which it could refer.
10 Dayānanda Sarasvatī justified Vedic sacrifices on environmental grounds: the burning of fragrant substances purifies the surrounding air, and the rising warm air promotes rain: Ghasi Ram, 1925: 63-75.
11 The form *prayatātmanaḥ* is grammatically masculine. But we are entitled to use the Pūrva Mīmāṃsā device of *ūha:* the extension of the application of a text to instances which are excluded by its grammatical form.
12 Edgerton uses this apt translation in 2.49.
13 This word is appropriate here rather than "person", because the *Gītā* uses male terms.
14 Note that it is possible to be self-centred even while worshipping God. The demonic man may offer much more than a leaf, a flower, a fruit or water, but he does not offer himself (cf. 9.26 discussed above).
15 This passage in the Īśā Up. is discussed in relation to the *Bhagavadgītā* by Paul Hacker, 1961: 365-99. The article in question has been translated by Dermot Killingley in W Halbfass (ed.), 1995: 273-318; the relevant pages are 281f.

6 Possessing the World: Wealth (artha) & the Bhagavadgītā

Ashis Gupta

Artha as "Wealth"

There is probably something mysterious, even fateful perhaps, in the process by which individuals acquire wealth. While scholars might justifiably pride themselves in being the custodian of *jñāna* or wisdom, we are far from unlocking the secret of generating wealth either at the societal level or the level of the individual. Wisdom tells us a great deal about the damaging, soul-destroying potential of wealth. The urgency of having to cope with our daily lives urges us to respect wealth, if not to pursue it with single-minded determination.

In so far as I believe that, in embracing the life of an academic rather than that of an ascetic, I have not succeeded in wholly renouncing the fruits of my desiring, perhaps I can claim some immunity against any charge of having imposed my own interpretative values on the subject of our discussion. The truth, however, is that I find in the *Bhagavadgītā* a perfectly plausible reconciliation between the goal of "salvation" and the burden of earthly existence. Therein lies the relevance of the *Gītā* to the concept of *artha*. And who can deny the relevance of *artha* to our times when it remains the perpetual quest of the governments we choose to elect and the children we bring into the world?

The *Bhagavadgītā* is quite unequivocal on the subject of wealth. In ch.16, Krishna paints a rather grim picture of those who lust after wealth:

> "They are bound by hundreds of vain hopes. Anger and lust is their refuge; and they strive by unjust means to amass wealth *(artha)* for their own cravings. 16.12.
>
> 'I have gained this today, and I shall attain this desire. This wealth is mine, and that shall also be mine.' 16.13."[1]

Krishna says: "In the vast cycles of life and death I inexorably hurl them down to destruction: these the lowest of men, cruel and evil, whose soul is hate" (16.19).

Traditionally, *artha* as a "goal of life" *(puruṣārtha)* may well have referred to the "wealth" or means required to sponsor a *yajña* or ritual sacrifice. But the meaning of the term may be extrapolated, I believe, to mean "wealth" in a modern sense. As I shall indicate, I believe this meaning is not alien to the spirit of the *Bhagavadgītā*, and it is this meaning that I shall explore in this essay.

If wealth is to be one of the fruits of our desiring, the *Gītā* leaves little doubt that it will lead to the path of perdition, unless there are more extenuating circumstances, that is, a conscious avoidance of desire, anger, and greed, the threefold gates of hell: "Work done for a reward is much lower than work done in the Yoga of wisdom. Seek salvation in the wisdom of reason. How poor those who work for a reward!" (2.49).

Artha and Dharma

Artha is not an isolated concept or object in the *Gītā*. Time and again, *artha* is woven into the concept of work or action *(karman)* and the concept of wisdom *(jñāna)*. *Jñāna*, on the other hand, is consistently contrasted with *karman*, pointing to the apperception of transcendent reality as distinct from the phenomenal world. This distinction is made possible through the workings of *buddhi* (or the judging intellect). These related concepts are critical in helping us reconcile with the fruits of our desiring. They help us find answers to two specific questions:

1) Do we turn away from these fruits? and
2) Do we let the fruits wither away on their branches?

The concept of *jñāna* plays an important role in our search for answers. Ch.7 of the *Gītā* contains a series of remarkable verses encouraging, applauding, and glorifying the "knower" or *jñānī*. Mascaro translates *jñānī* as "the man of vision". Krishna makes a distinction between "the man of vision" and "the seeker of something he treasures", when he says: "There are four kinds of men who are good, and the four love me, Arjuna: the man of sorrows *(ārta),* the seeker of knowledge *(jijñāsu),* the seeker of something he treasures *(arthārthī),* and the man of vision *(jñānī)"* (7.16). He goes on to say:

> "The greatest of these is the man of vision, who is ever one, who loves the One. For I love the man of vision, and the man of vision loves me" (7.17).

While we are all engaged in the pursuit of *artha* in varying degrees, I am tempted to pose the question: "Are the great builders of vast industrial empires not visionaries in their own right?" — visionaries who have created substance where there was no substance, wealth where there was no wealth? Although my answer is "yes", I must add that, consistent with the spirit of the *Gītā,* it is not an unqualified "yes". Just as nothing in the *Gītā* is unqualified, I too would say "yes" only if these visionaries can be perceived as having steered clear of desire, anger, and greed — the threefold gates of hell.

According to Rāmānuja, *jñānī* in this context is "the man who knows that the eternal self is totally different from material nature, who desires the Lord and considers Him to be the final goal".[2] I cannot see Rāmānuja's or anybody else's translation as excluding creators of wealth from the ranks of the worthy — assuming, of course, that "they desire the Lord and consider Him to be the final goal". My own research on Indian entrepreneurs points to a significant number, albeit of an earlier generation, who regard themselves as transient custodians of material wealth and who are often imbued with a powerful sense of social responsibility.

Modern attitudes to Artha

In trying to explore *artha* from our own present perspective, I believe it would be reasonably safe to say that no one is present in this Conference without a certain level of access to wealth either directly or through parents or grandparents. Whether we have seriously derived it ourselves or not, wealth is certainly a highly desirable commodity. Bernard Shaw recreates a formidable paradox in "Mrs Warren's Profession" where Mrs Warren's daughter gains access to culture and high education through the spoils of Mrs Warren's questionable profession wherein she catered to the fruits of other people's desiring.

However desirable *artha* may be, our own generation has expressed considerable ambivalence towards it. On the one hand we have unblushing votaries of the Friedmanesque ilk: Margaret Thatcher, Ronald Reagan and the like. On the other side, the twentieth century has been bedevilled by the spirit of Marx who equated wealth with power by insisting with an alarming relevance that production is dominated by those who control and supply capital, and that their numbers are continually diminishing as more and more monopolies are set up.

Our ambivalence probably stems from the different ways wealth has been defined in different societies at different times, and the lamentable fallouts from its use in almost every case. Today, as much as in earlier times, *artha* as a fruit of our desiring can leave behind sad consequences which become a pox on our social order. Thus a complex web of wealth, technology, high population growth, low mortality rates, and other factors may be seen as responsible for the awesome poverty in parts of Asia and Africa, and even the bedrock poverty in many developed nations. While corporations reap record profits, the poor get poorer. Some say they get poorer because they are elderly and inflation erodes their savings, because they are unskilled and can't compete in the job market, or technology has rendered their skills obsolete. For others, poverty is simply the bitter legacy of several centuries of bigotry — the fruit of persistent and systematic prejudice against racial, religious, and ethnic minorities in education, housing and employment, not to mention centuries of colonial exploitation.

While our own times tend to equate wealth with capital or money, other societies have seen fit to equate wealth with cattle, produce and wives, but most significantly, with land. A belief in land as wealth is an interesting case in point because of what it spat out in the process of pursuing and devouring the fruits of its desiring. As J Galbraith points out in his *The New Industrial State:*

> "The eminence of capital is a relatively recent matter; until about two centuries ago no perceptive man would have doubted that power was decisively associated with land.....For three and a half centuries after the discovery of America appreciation of the strategic importance of land gave it an even greater role in history".[3]

One of the most enduring definitions of wealth was formulated by Cambridge University's Professor Joan Robinson who wrote:

> "Economic wealth is not a very precise idea and we must be content with a rough definition of it. Broadly, economic wealth is the *command* over goods and services that are desired, or consuming power for short".[4]

Dwelling on this definition for a moment, it takes less than profound insight to observe that "consuming power" may be possessed at a subsistence level or at a gargantuan level. At the subsistence level, there is unlikely to be any surplus left for an individual or their family. At the end of the day, does this "subsistence person" have any wealth left? The answer is, None. Now let us assume for a moment that a man with a gargantuan consuming power strives for, and actually succeeds in achieving, command over a vast array of goods and services. But then he allows his consumption to slide to the subsistence level. Lucky man! What he is left with is an enormous surplus. Indeed it may be argued that he would never find himself in a "commanding" position if he had not succeeded in creating in the first place at least a little surplus, just a little capital, by somehow restraining his appetite, by leaving untouched at least a portion of the fruits of his desiring. Does this man meet the *Gītā's* test of *artha* that will not drag one down to hell?

Wealth and Detachment

What the *Gītā* has to say on the subject of *artha* has provoked the interest of countless commentators. I have neither aspired to, nor perhaps succeeded in discovering, any insights which might have escaped earlier scholars. Indeed, the task I set myself was a simple one, reflecting the overall theme of the Conference: the ethics and relevance of the *Bhagavadgītā* for our times. I asked myself a very naive question: in considering the subject of *artha* is it possible to have your cake and eat it? And perhaps derive a modicum of pleasure in the process?

Over and over again, Krishna demands that one should give up all *attachment* to works *and* their fruits. If we are to lend our ears to Krishna's exhortations we may well ask: Then why work? The paradox inherent in this situation is perfectly expressed in the structure of the second discourse where we find a sharp shift from a purely practical argument aimed at persuading Arjuna to go to war to a consideration of the contemplative life by which Arjuna will put away the bondage that is inherent in all work:

> "This is the wisdom of Sankhya — the vision of the Eternal. Hear now the wisdom of Yoga, path of the Eternal and freedom from bondage" (2.39).

Although the subject of *artha* may be seen as one of the many paradoxes embedded in the *Bhagavadgītā,* it would seem that the path to resolving the paradox is also laid out before our eyes. While Krishna urges Arjuna to action against his kinsmen, nowhere is action commanded for its own sake. Human beings, it is suggested, must never be committed to any action, however apparently worthwhile — one may only use works *(karman)* as a means to transcending works themselves, for "works" of their very nature "bind". The way the *Gītā* offers us a way out of the paradox is this: when Arjuna argues against fighting his kinsmen on ethical grounds, Krishna responds with metaphysical arguments. Likewise, *artha* may also be legitimised if its pursuit is characterised by essential renunciation. This may seem logically an absurdity except that, at a metaphysical level, such a detachment is a necessary condition for *mokṣa* or release from the bondage of rebirth.

Simply desiring *artha* is one thing, pursuing it with determination is something else. The modest goal of merely desiring can be accomplished through an essentially passive role, a condition not commended by the *Gītā:* "Not by refraining from action does a man attain freedom from action. Not by mere renunciation does he attain supreme perfection" (3.4). But the pursuit of wealth demands "action", and nowhere does the *Gītā* stigmatise the creation of wealth as a roguish activity. While it is sometimes unclear in ch. 18 where Kṣatriyas acquire *artha* to enable them to be generous and possess a lordly mien, the natural activities of Vaiśyas are certainly legitimised: to till the fields, protect the cattle, and engage in trade are the works of peasants and artisans, inhering in their nature.

According to Śaṃkara, Brahmins originate from Goodness *(sattva),* Kṣatriyas from Passion *(rajas)* mixed with Goodness, peasants and artisans from Passion mixed with Darkness *(tamas),* and Śūdras from Darkness with a small admixture of Passion.[5] Ch.14 expounds on Goodness, Passion and Darkness (or Light, Fire and Darkness as translated by Mascaro) — the three *guṇa*s or constituents sprung from Nature *(prakṛti)* that bind the (embodied) self to the body. *Sattva* causes the self to cling to wisdom and to joy. *Rajas* is instinct with desire and causes the embodied self to cling to works. And *tamas* is from ignorance born. Clearly, Śaṃkara didn't think too highly of Vaiśyas.

Interestingly, Rāmānuja believed one's caste as being predetermined by one's former lives.[6] This observation is fraught with serious implications for *artha.* The observation makes it imperative upon us to adhere to the numberless injunctions arising from work, renunciation, and sacrifice, or risk drifting further and further away from the attainment of salvation. Lest we forget, and this discussion becomes an exercise in futility, let me draw your attention to the fact that the entire ethical framework of the *Bhagavadgītā* is predicated on the assumption of one's seeking "salvation" or liberation as number one priority in life. Take away that ultimate fruit of our desiring — eternal liberation — and the entire structure disintegrates. Indeed, men and women realise their most cherished goals through a process of integration, integration of moral principles with practical goals:

> "But great is the man who, free from attachments, and with a mind ruling its powers in harmony, works on the path of Karma Yoga, the path of consecrated action" (3.7).

The End of Artha

Eternal liberation must then be the ultimate quest. All trace of being an ego, all trace of *possessing* anything at all must be ruthlessly swept away, if the true self is to return to its spiritual home, Nirvāṇa which is Brahman too:

> "This is the Eternal in man, O Arjuna. Reaching him all delusion is gone. Even in the last hour of his life upon earth, man can reach the Nirvana of Brahman — man can find peace in the peace of his God" (2.72).

After all, as Krishna reminds us,

> "The Yogi works for the purification of the soul, he throws off selfish attachment, and thus it is only his body or his senses or his mind or his reason that works.
> This man of harmony surrenders the reward of his work and thus attains final peace.
> The man of disharmony, urged by desire, is attached to his rewards and remains in bondage" (5.11-12).

What the *Bhagavadgītā* does is transfer the cycle of human life and death from an earthly plane to a cosmic plane. If that is indeed the moral system that we choose to subscribe to, then all other temporal sub-systems must seem relatively unimportant. The fruits of our desiring become less important than our salvation. Except for the fruit of salvation, all other fruits have their own cycles of transience and perishability. Where the cycle of our lives meets the cycles of the fruits of our desiring remains a mystery. We are at liberty to seize the fruits, we may use them, sacrifice them, give them away, but the fruits have their own ebb and flow, their inscrutable randomness. So we are told: "Do thy work in the peace of Yoga and, free from selfish desires, be not moved in success or in failure. Yoga is evenness of mind — a peace that is ever the same" (2.48). And, as a salutary reminder to those who may be puffed with pride at their own brilliance, the *Gītā* says:

> "All actions take place in time by the interweaving of the forces of Nature; but the man lost in selfish delusion thinks that he himself is the actor". (3.27)

In surrendering we ensure plenty:

> "Thus spoke the Lord of Creation when he made both man and sacrifice: By sacrifice thou shalt multiply and obtain all thy desires" (3.10).

This may seem a rather odd way to generate surplus. However, certain contemporary economists also hold the view that there are two ways of satisfying desires. One is to want more and the other is to want less. In fact, even under capitalistic rules of the game, a major part of production is for sale, not for consumption. Therefore desire is perhaps a necessary spur to wealth creation. Combined with self-denial and renunciation, what this creates is a kind of surplus, "fruits" that we are able to, or prepared to, transcend.

Even without the benefit of complex economic theories, Krishna was wise enough to realise the immense and wide-ranging implications of work *(karman)*. While work is persistently encouraged, there is a realisation underlying the four great classes of society that not all work can be productive. Let us consider a social model where there is a single Brahmin and a single Kṣatriya — two individuals in all. Let us call this a transactional model where the generous prince gives and gives continually. All other things being equal, there is no invader threatening to blow up the castle, and life seems pretty easy. For his part, the Brahmin dutifully carves out sacrificial rites pouring *ghee* and grains in the sacred fire. Mind you, there's nobody to milk the cows or harvest the grain. So, in theory at least, the only way the model can acquire even a semblance of equilibrium is if there's a Vaiśya around.

This third new member of our model presumably tills the soil and, somewhere along the line, in pursuit of the fruits of his desiring, acquires a wife whom he promptly sends out to milk the cows. Now in pursuit of the fruits of their mutual desiring, these two bring forth little Vaiśyas into the world. This, of course, complicates the model. Both adult Vaiśyas find themselves saddled with exacting full-time jobs. Who's to deliver the milk? Who's to carry the grain to the prince? Life is becoming too stressful; domestic violence is lurking beneath the surface, and there's no psychiatrist around (yet). Clearly, the model is in desperate need of a fourth member — the Śūdra. The world of the *Bhagavadgītā* had succeeded in creating an unsurpassable economic model. Unfortunately, it had also given rise to a fresh problematic. This becomes evident when Krishna tells Arjuna that it would be in vain for him to think of *not* engaging in battle. His *nature* would compel him. Krishna goes on to say:

> "Because thou art in the bondage of Karma, of the forces of thine own past life, and that which thou, in thy delusion, with a good will dost not want to do, unwillingly thou shalt have to do" (18.60).

Artha and Poverty

The introduction of the Śūdra in our economic model fills many of us with unease and foreboding, especially when set against the concept of the bondage of karma. I am thus led to at least a limited discussion of poverty without which any exploration of *artha* would be sadly incomplete. While the *Gītā's* injunctions regarding the four classes of society might go a long way towards securing a social stability of sorts, there's no denying that, within the context of democratic thought, they help institutionalise structural poverty to a certain extent and tend to mediate against any notions of affirmative action and upward social mobility. "Perform therefore thy task in life" (3.2), says Krishna.

I have tried, like Arjuna, to find a way out of this cruel dilemma. The closest escape that I have found is simply one of consolation. This idea of consolation is inextricably linked with notions of *bhakti* and sacrifice:

> "But to those who adore me with a pure oneness of soul, to those who are ever in harmony, I increase what they have and I give them what they have not" (9.22).

Krishna promises to accept the devotion of the poor and dispossessed as gladly as he would do from others:

> "He who offers to me with devotion only a leaf, or a flower, or a fruit, or even a little water, this I accept from that yearning soul, because with a poor heart it was offered with love" (9.26).

I must concede that it is difficult for us, towards the end of the twentieth century, to accept in principle a world governed by rules of predestination. But could the reason for this be that we are accustomed to perceiving our lives only in a temporal plane? Could this reason lie in our inability to project our expectations to the world beyond, promised in the *Gītā*? Through some of the most poetic words I have ever come across, the *Gītā* tells us: "At the end of the night of time all things return to my nature; and when the new day of time begins I bring them again into light" (9.7).

If we look at the reality of democratic principles, we must realise that democracy, in its modern meanings, began as a system which gave the suffrage to those who had proved their worth by acquiring real property, and to no others. Quite apart from this detail, it is perhaps fair to say that, for close to one-half of the world's population (now nearing the 6 billion mark), freedom and democratic choice remain mere illusions, hollow mantras that produce no magic. The predestined reality of the *Bhagavadgītā* is probably closest to their present and future status.

ARTHA AND THE FUTURE

One important fact should not be overlooked in this system: the sense of predestination inherent in caste thrusts our actions, once again, from a comprehensible temporal plane to a potentially fragile cosmic plane. In other words, we are held accountable not only for the duration of our forseeable life, but also the unforseeable duration of our future incarnations. There is always the danger of sliding deeper towards hell.

In conclusion, let me say that the pursuit of surplus-generating wealth today is far more complex than the pursuit simply of the generalised fruits of our desiring. A hundred years ago a capacity to create wealth necessitated not only access to capital, but also imagination and a propensity towards decisiveness and risk. All these elements must have been part of the primitive economic model we discussed earlier. Unbeknownst to him — or maybe he knew it all too well — Krishna had stumbled upon a vital economic principle that took 2000 years or more to be set into a modern context by Paul Samuelson. I am referring to what have been called the factors of production — land, labour, capital, and the entrepreneurial talent that brings these together — and Samuelson's comment: "But, at any time, there will be a maximum obtainable amount of product for any given amounts of factor inputs".[7]

With our own societies awash with labour, much of it unwanted and technologically irrelevant, *artha* as a fruit of our desiring seems increasingly beyond the reach of millions. Under such circumstances, any suggestion about the relevance of yoga and karmic values might quickly be laughed at as another prescription for an opiate of the masses. Today we need a new factor of production. What we need might be considered a fresh talent for bringing together men and women of diverse technical knowledge and experience. We need persons of vision — *jñānīs* — to be able to do this, and the *Bhagavadgītā* would praise such to the sky.

Even as the locus of wealth and wealth-creation shifts dramatically from land to capital to organised competence, the *Gītā* remains supremely relevant in its established checks and balances that ensure spiritual and social harmony, and offer protection against economic exploitation, environmental degradation, and even mindless military aggression. Of course, in the end, all these several and many injunctions are mere words, and one may consign them to the fire as we are urged to consign our works to the fire of sacrifice so splendidly described by Krishna: "Even as a burning fire burns all fuel to ashes, the fire of eternal wisdom burns into ashes all works" (4.37).

But the spirit of the *Bhagavadgītā* is imperishable, precisely because its ultimate message is so simple. Pursue the fruits of your desiring if you will, but stay a "moral" course bereft of hypocrisy, duplicity, greed, arrogance, and cruelty. Pursue lives that do not abuse your own inherent nobility as embodiments of the eternal spirit, lives that do not debase this nobility in others.

1 Translations are quoted from J Mascaro, 1962. Similarly, in 16.12, *artha* is translated as "wealth" by e.g. Zaehner, Sargeant, van Buitenen and W Johnson in their renditions of the *Gītā.*
2 See R C Zaehner, 1969: 250.
3 J K Galbraith, 1979: 53.
4 J Robinson, 1965: 15. It is worth noting that Joan Robinson has also stated that "One of the great metaphysical ideas in economics is expressed by the word 'value'", 1962: 26.
5 See R C Zaehner, op.cit., p.393.
6 R C Zaehner, ibid.
7 P Samuelson, 1976: 537

Transcending the World?: Freedom (mokṣa) & the Bhagavadgītā

Will Johnson

Arjuna's Dilemma

At the beginning of the *Bhagavadgītā* Arjuna is faced by a problem — the problem of how to choose rightly when faced by a number of apparently incompatible routes or solutions.[1] Perhaps it is a question which our own age has been confronted with in an acute form, from "consumer choice" to multiple "universes of discourse" and "alternative", not to say "virtual" realities. It is of course possible not to see this as a problem at all. Some cultural relativists and post-modernists simply glory in the multiplicity of it all, propounding neither a solution nor a criterion for making the right choice but simply asserting the undesirability, perhaps even the impossibility, of rational choice. This, however, is more of a cultural stance than a prescription for conducting one's everyday life, where practical choices have continually to be made.

Of course, the kinds of multiple choices we face in day to day existence are for the most part trivial — "life-style" choices — and few suppose they can liberate us from anything more significant than inconvenience or boredom. The choice disabling Arjuna at the beginning of the *Gītā* is of a different order, for it seems to him that his actions will have not only immediate effects but also long-term soteriological consequences. Underlying this view is, of course, the law of karma, which holds that significant actions, perhaps all actions, have positive or negative results for the actor. How he chooses to act seems to Arjuna therefore to be of paramount importance. His dilemma springs from the incompatibility between, on the one hand, the universal yet individual renouncer-ethic of non-violence and non-engagement, and on the other, the particularistic Brahminical ethic of engagement with the world in the light of one's pre-defined social responsibility or *sva-dharma.* In the terms of the former, the latter will bring bad soteriological results. Renouncers renounce the world precisely in order to transcend it in the very concrete sense of achieving ultimate liberation from suffering and rebirth, i.e. from the effects of their karma. In the light of this, the Brahminical sva-dharmic system seems at best no solution at all.

There are, of course, good historical reasons why this particular problem arises when it does, and why in the *Gītā* it is necessary to find a solution to it, which I shall not go into here.[2] Suffice it to say that by proposing that the route to liberation requires *internal* renunciation, viz. renunciation of attachment to, or desire for, the results of one's actions, combined with external adherence to one's inherent duty *(sva-dharma),* the *Gītā* effects a compromise, which is externally or socially conservative, but internally radical.

What I shall explore at greater length in this paper is the rationale for this compromise: why it is not presented as just one more choice, albeit the best or most highly recommended, but instead comes effectively to be seen as *the only possible solution,* because it is the only one which accords with the way things really are. In other words, I shall argue that, faced with what is, in soteriological terms, an apparently crucial problem of choice — an ethical dilemma — the *Gītā* adopts, through Krishna, a strategy which is effectively the very opposite of that espoused by contemporary cultural relativists. Far from there being an almost infinite number of equally valid options, the *Gītā* demonstrates that, in the light of reality, choice is no longer possible in any meaningful sense — that is to say, there is only *one* valid response.

At one level this is, of course, to overstate the case, since it is evident that one *can* choose, if only to acknowledge or deny that no choice is possible. But clearly, in the light of Krishna's teaching, whatever the theoretical choice, there is in fact only one possible way to act, and that both reflects and is a consequence of the way things really are *(dharma).* So perhaps it is more precise to say that there is, in a strictly literal sense, a real choice in the *Gītā,* but it is not between renunciation of the world and engagement in it, rather, it is between acknowledging one's *lack* of real choice and remaining ignorant of that fact (in so far as ignorance of something can be deemed a choice). As we shall see, acknowledgement entails almost ineluctable consequences in terms of the way one behaves, and it is those two together — knowledge of the way things really are and acting in accordance with that knowledge — which are the ultimate liberating factors in the *Gītā.*

So let me begin by considering briefly the way the world is according to the *Gītā,* viz. Krishna, and how this dictates individual action. I shall then go on to look at the relation of both to liberation or freedom.

Reality and Action

According to Krishna, the world is action-bound and action-driven; so it is impossible not to act. One should not, however, act for personal ends; rather, one should act without attachment to the results and simply for the maintenance of the world (ch.3 *passim).* Indeed, this is the way Krishna himself acts. There is more to it than this, however. In the great theophany of ch.11, it becomes clear that Krishna is in reality the *only* real actor — human beings are merely his instruments and entirely subject to his will (11.32-34). The point is made again, less dramatically, in the final chapter:

"Arjuna, in the centre of the heart of all beings their lord stands still, mechanically revolving all creatures through his magical power" (18.61).[3]

And the following verse provides a logical and soteriological corollary to this insight:

> "Bharata, go with your whole being to him alone for refuge; through his grace you will reach supreme peace, eternal home" (18.62).

One consequence of this view is that the way the world is and the way people are is inevitably the way the world and people should be. In other words, the socio-religious system that the *Gītā* proposes is God-validated; *dharma* is therefore not a matter of choice but pre-ordained and prescribed. Or as Patrick Olivelle has put it, "It is.....choice in matters of *dharma* — the very choice that Arjuna had decided to exercise in deciding not to fight — that Krishna is attempting to combat".[4] As I have already suggested, the way Krishna deals with this is to teach, and then demonstrate, that individual choice is essentially an illusion, since God is the only real chooser, God is the only real actor.

But where, apart from out in the cold, does this leave free-will, and an individual's attempts to exercise choice or free-will in the attempt to achieve spiritual liberation? In other words, where does the *Gītā* stand on the question of action *(karman)* and its effects? As we have seen, all actions are essentially God's actions and all effects or "fruits" are likewise his. For humans to "act" out of desire for results (soteriological or otherwise) is therefore to make a mistake about the real identity of the agent — or so it seems. But perhaps it is not really a mistake. Could it not be claimed that in the *Gītā* the individual and God are essentially identical, and therefore the individual is autonomous in karmic terms?

The Gītā: theistic or monistic?

The arguments over whether the *Gītā* is ultimately theistic or absolutistic/monistic are well known, and well known to be unresolved. Indeed, since they involve assumptions exterior to the text itself, they are probably not capable of resolution in any universally acceptable sense.[5] I do not want to rehearse such arguments here. Nevertheless, I find it difficult to resist the conclusion that the *soteriologically* significant God in the *Gītā* is more personal than impersonal, more *saguṇa* than *nirguṇa*. I would further suggest that in editorial terms, this precedence of a personal God over the impersonal Brahman is achieved through that process of hierarchical "trumping" or inclusivism[6] so familiar to students of Indian religions. This is a process which, at the level of primary texts, tends to mirror, in an almost linear fashion, wider historical developments. So, for instance, the Brahman of the early Upaniṣads is likely to be "trumped" by the personal gods of the later flowering *bhakti* and Tantric traditions. Perhaps in the case of the *Gītā* as we now have it, this inclusivism represents the scriptural hardening of what, textually and theologically speaking, had previously been a more fluid oral tradition. At the commentarial level, as opposed to that of the text itself, the position remains fluid: earlier commentators are subject to sophisticated theological "trumping" by their successors.

However, it is with the text as we have it that I am currently concerned, and my argument in short is that *bhakti,* whether the latest addition to that text or not, is the *Gītā's* overriding soteriological principle. *Bhakti* is placed at the top of the hierarchy and all other means are its subordinates. Others, of course, might, by a further inclusivist manoeuvre, subordinate *bhakti* to a monistic absolutism,[7] but I repeat that my concern here is not with the theoretical question of whether the God of the *Gītā* is *ultimately nirguṇa* or *saguṇa* (which clearly cannot be answered on the basis of the text itself), rather it is with the practicalities of the path to liberation, which I believe to be the *Gītā's* own major concern.

In short, it seems to me that the argument that the individual and God are identical in the *Gītā* can only be sustained by a reading which subordinates the practical religious implications of Krishna's theophany in ch.11, and the specific recommendation of *bhakti* and reliance on God's grace or action as the essential routes to liberation, to a more abstract and theoretical reading.[8] In this connection it is worth quoting Richard Gombrich's answer to a question which he calls "crucial for Indian thinking", namely, "just what is meant by being the agent of an act?":

> "Every Indian who learnt Sanskrit.....did so from Panini's grammar, which defines the agent as independent. In the earlier period of Hindu theism the soul is ultimately identical with God, at least in most respects, so that the individual can be a true agent: his agency and God's coincide, to the derogation of neither. In Ramanuja God transcends his devotees; He is master, they are slaves and own nothing. God is the only true agent. What we call "human effort" is just a form of God's power . Fatalism returns through a theistic backdoor".[9]

As I have already made clear, it is not my intention in this paper to enter the lists on behalf of, or even to review particular sectarian commentaries on, the *Gītā,* important as these are for our understanding of its development as a key text in the history of Indian religions. Nevertheless, it seems to me that in terms of his total and overriding agency, the Krishna of the *Gītā* is very difficult to distinguish from Rāmānuja's God, as depicted, in this instance, by Gombrich. Indeed, perhaps the *Gītā* itself is a watershed not just for the attribution of agency but for the perceived effectiveness of the law of karma and its manipulation as a means to liberation in Hindu theistic traditions.

The Gītā and Free Will

In the light of this, it is instructive to turn the question inside out and ask not "how is one liberated according to the *Gītā*?", but "how is it possible *not* to be liberated according to the *Gītā*?". This can be explored briefly by looking at a number of verses from ch.9. Krishna begins by telling Arjuna that what he has to relate is "the most secret knowledge and insight" (9.1); however, men who have no faith in this truth — this *dharma* — fail to reach Krishna and are returned to *saṃsāra*.They go on dying. For those who are ignorant of Krishna's higher state as lord of creatures, and so of their total dependency upon him (9.11; cf.9.4-10), all hopes, actions and knowledge are futile (9.12). On the other hand, those who do know Krishna's true nature, those who do have faith in the teaching which reveals it, and worship him single-mindedly (9.13), go to him (9.25ff). In fact, since Krishna *is* everything (9.16-18), it is very difficult not to worship him. And indeed, there are those who worship him in an accidental or involuntary fashion, in the belief that they are worshipping or sacrificing to someone else (9.23). But because they do not truly recognise him, they slide (9.24) — that is to say, they do not achieve the full soteriological effect. And now it is made clear that it is devotion to Krishna alone which brings liberation or freedom, which here is designated as "coming" to Krishna (9.28, 9.34). Significantly, this kind of single-minded devotion brings "liberation from good and evil results, from the bonds of action *(karman)*" (9.28). This is not to say that various kinds of yogic practices do not serve a propaedeutic function, but ultimately it is those who depend on Krishna who "go by the highest path" (9.32), and such devotion is sufficient of itself: no devotee of Krishna is lost (9.31).

The short answer to the question, therefore, is that through ignorance of Krishna's true nature and its unwitting, deficient, or misdirected devotion, it is all too easy not to be liberated. Clearly, the expectation is that, once one has been made privy to the *Gītā's* teaching, there is no real possibility that one could be perverse enough to persist in one's misdirection. Nevertheless, an element of free will seems to be allowed here (albeit in the context of there being only one *appropriate* choice), i.e. one can choose between liberating knowledge and devotion, and non-liberating ignorance and its corollaries. Of course, from the perspective revealed by the theophany of ch.11, Krishna himself has already determined this outcome as well: if one is perverse, if one dies again and again, ultimately that is because Krishna wills it. In one's actions one is merely the instrument of God's will — karma as an independent mechanism or law of nature is superseded. Liberation is effectively in the gift of God, who it seems can be swayed by the degree of one's devotion or conformity to his will.

It is instructive to examine this tension between free will and God's will (or necessity) in a little more detail. Essentially, the *Gītā* presents a reformulation of the problem of fate versus human effort, determinism versus free will, which lies at the heart of the *Mahābhārata* as a whole. Zaehner summarises this relationship for us:

> "Though the Mahābhārata stresses time and again the primacy of fate over human effort, it none the less compares the two to the rain which prepares the ground and the seed that man puts into it (5.78.2-5): the two are interdependent and work in harmony together. Human *karma* is but a fraction of the *karma* of the whole universe, and this totality of *karma* adds up to fate, and fate itself is under the control of God. Fate is the cosmic *dharma* from which man cannot escape; and in the long run it is man's co-operation with fate which is but another word for God's will that justifies him and earns him a place in heaven or that causes him to enter into God".[10]

This seems very similar to the position in the *Gītā* (perhaps Zaehner had the *Gītā* in mind when he formulated it). But the *Gītā* differs from its parent epic in the role it allots to Krishna, or perhaps one should say, Krishna allots himself. Dr John D Smith has remarked that:

> "One of the most important ways in which Fate manifests itself in the *Mahābhārata* is in the person of Kṛṣṇa. If the cosmic plan is likened to a drama, then Kṛṣṇa is the stage-manager: abstaining from an active part, particularly in the fighting, he nonetheless guides the Pāṇḍavas along the paths they have to take.....He is thus, in a sense, Fate's own representative in the action which Fate has instigated, simultaneously involved in events and aloof from them".[11]

As Dr Smith also remarks, Krishna is much more than just Fate's stage-manager. "He is also.....the great god of the epic, Viṣṇu incarnate" (op.cit., p.72), but perhaps the full implications of this for human action are spelt out only in the *Gītā*. Indeed, the principal difference between this Krishna and the Krishna of the *Gītā* is that the latter, while in the dramatic context refraining from significant action yet again, reveals himself to be the *only* real actor. For instance, it would be impossible in the context of the *Gītā,* where Krishna is "time run on, destroyer of the universe" (11.32), to imagine a verse such as the following, which occurs as part of a long discourse on fate and human effort in the *Sauptikaparvan* of the epic: "Human effort, once undertaken, succeeds through fate, and then the result of that action accrues to the agent".[12]

Clearly the agent referred to here is not fate but the human who has made the effort. In the *Gītā,* however, Krishna subsumes within himself both fate and agency, and as a result all that is left to humans is correctly to attribute the results of their apparent actions to the real agent. In other words, the dichotomy between fate, identified as past karma (the passive aspect), and human effort (the active corollary),[13] is collapsed, for according to the *Gītā* all karma, past, present and future, is God's alone.[14]

What becomes clear from considering this question is that, if karma is understood as the sum of an individual agent's actions and their results, its significance as a means to liberation is attenuated to the point of irrelevance in the *Gītā.* Certainly the classical view of the individual as subject to rebirth in *saṃsāra* is retained and referred to, but the manipulation of the law of karma as a means of release from that cycle is rejected. In its place we have God's universal agency, and its corollary, *bhakti.* In these new circumstances, the currency of liberation is not karma but, in the first place, knowledge — knowledge of that divine total agency, and the consequent total dependency of human beings in the realm of action — and, in the second place, the acting out of that dependence through devotion. As we saw in ch.9.28, the bonds of action, good and evil results, are not destroyed by further actions or inaction, but by one particular "action": devotion. In practical terms, this entails turning over the results of one's actions to the real actor, God, and relying entirely on his liberating power. This is spelt out, almost as an afterthought, in the final chapter of the *Gītā,* but the trajectory of what has gone before, and particularly the theophany of ch.11, ensures that it is hardly a surprising conclusion, even though billed as the "mystery of mysteries" (18.63).

It is of course true that verse by verse, and chapter by chapter, the *Gītā* rehearses a complex of possible soteriological means and goals.[15] So for instance, for the ritualist (i.e. the motivated actor, who as agent desires the results of his actions) the goal is heaven or a long life, which, like the effects of his actions, are impermanent. For both the *jñāna-yogin,* the knower-renouncer, and the *karma-yogin,* the internal renouncer, the goal is the *nirvāṇa* of *brahman (brahma-nirvāṇa).* For the *bhakta* or devotee (who is also an internal renouncer), the goal is, as we have seen, God (Krishna). Viewed as a whole,[16] however, the text does not treat these means and ends as equally valid options. The ritualists' heaven is discredited by its impermanence, and Brahman is subsumed under Krishna.[17] In short, just as the fact of God and the way that he is (revealed in his theophany) mean that there is only one real goal, one kind of freedom, so God's agency and its requirement of *bhakti* overrule or subsume all other means to that freedom. As the final chapter of the *Gītā* puts it, having become Brahman through achieving the highest state of knowledge (18.50), which is synonymous with attaining "the supreme perfection of freedom from action and its results through renunciation" of the fruits of action (18.49), one attains the highest devotion to Krishna (18.54). And then, to quote directly: "Through devotion (a man) recognises me — how great I am, and who I am in reality; and then having known me in reality, he enters me immediately" (18.55).

Through Krishna's grace such a man "attains the eternal, imperishable home" (18.56; cf.18.62). What kind of state this is, is unexplained, and perhaps inexplicable; it is simply taken for granted that it is the highest goal. It is clear, however, that God remains immeasurably greater than the liberated soul, and this, in a rather unsettling way, introduces a hint of uncertainty. God has promised liberation to the devotee, he has even said that the devotee (or Arjuna standing in for the devotee) is dear to him (18.65). Nevertheless, liberation is ultimately dependent upon God's grace alone. Unlike for those systems (whether sacrificial or soteriological) which depend upon the strict operation of the law, viz. the mechanism of karma, the *Gītā's* goal is never guaranteed simply by conforming to the prescribed pattern of behaviour.

That is not to say that you can achieve the goal *without* conforming to that pattern, but the removal of human agency has made the result uncertain, in the sense that there is no *automatic* or necessary causal connection between behaviour and result. Actions have results, but neither the actions nor the results are really ours. And that goes for the one result that really matters as well: liberation is no longer the result of human action — it is totally dependent on God's grace. The door is thereby opened to the full flowering of a religion based on devotion, faith and hope. The important thing about this in social terms, of course, is that it is a religion which can be practised *in* the world. No special conditions are required, there is no mechanism of karma to be manipulated in highly regulated monastic or renunciatory circumstances. Indeed, no special qualifications are required; it can be practised by virtually anyone (9.32), although it certainly helps to be a Brahmin (9.33). As Halbfass puts it: "(The *Gītā's*) soteriology of devotion avoids all exclusivism and restrictive legalism".[18]

I must now finally address the question of whether, or in what sense, the freedom or *mokṣa* the *Gītā* teaches entails transcendence of that world in which the way to it is mapped out, and the ethical implications of this.

The End of the Gītā and its Means

If by karma we mean the mechanism by which an individual is soteriologically conditioned by the results of his or her actions *in the world*, it is clear that the *Gītā's* teaching leads to the transcendence of karma. Actions in general have results but, given the right attitude to them, not soteriological ones. There is, however, a strong admonition that actions undertaken in the world should conform in all instances to the particularistic ethics which define one's *sva-dharma*. The world is willy-nilly a realm of karma, of action, according to Krishna, but the necessity for the kind of all-embracing, ethically defined codes of conduct that heterodox renouncer-traditions, such as Jainism and Buddhism, predicate on this given, is by-passed in the *Gītā* through the attribution of the consequences of action to God alone. So rather than all action being, at some level, soteriologically significant, the *Gītā* teaches virtually the opposite: that all action — action in itself — is soteriologically *insignificant*, with the proviso, of course, that the underlying attitude of non-attachment prevails in all cases. It is therefore perhaps not too simplistic to say that in the *Gītā* karma is transcended as a negative force, and its positive potential is subsumed within devotion to Krishna (i.e., positive acknowledgement of his universal agency). So if by "the world" we mean the world of apparent cause and effect, then certainly liberation, as defined by the *Gītā*, entails transcendence of the world. But because of the revelation of Krishna as universal agent and universal God, the devotee (represented by Arjuna in the great theophany of ch.11) views the world not so much as transcended but as transformed. With his divine eye, he sees the way the world really is — subsumed within and driven by God. Indeed, it is *only* by devotion that one can see God, i.e., the world transformed in this way:

> "Neither through the Vedas, nor through asceticism, neither by alms-giving, nor by sacrifice, is it possible to see me in the way you have seen me.
> But by exclusive devotion, Arjuna, I can be known and seen thus, as I really am, and entered into, Incinerator of the foe.
> He who acts for me, who makes me the highest goal, who is devoted to me, who has abandoned attachment, who is without hatred for any being, comes to me, Pāṇḍava" (11.53-55).

This indeed is a world in which *bhakti* and *dharma*, devotion and the true law, are synonymous:

> "Even the evil-doer, if he shares in me with single-minded devotion, may be thought of as good, for he has fixed on what is right.
> He quickly attains to the true law and attains everlasting peace....." (9.30-31).

What are the implications for contemporary ethical behaviour of this view of the world? In so far as the particularistic ethic of *sva-dharma* operates in the world of action, to that extent the person who transcends the world through devotion also transcends that ethic. But according to the *Gītā* he cannot, *while* he is the world, abandon it. Rather, he must process it through the internal attitude of non-attachment, or, perhaps more positively, selflessness. It is clearly not the *Gītā's* intention, therefore, that just any action done without attachment to the fruits is acceptable. Indeed, what is acceptable is defined in terms of the ideal status quo, namely, *sva-dharma*. B Matilal, writing of the epic as a whole, puts this in rather a seductive way, identifying Krishna as the paradigmatic "imaginative poet" who "looks at the particularity of the situation but also looks beyond it", allowing for "flexibility in *dharma*".[19] He goes on to say:

> "But this flexibility never means the "anything goes" kind of morality. He is the *poet* who accepts the constraints of metres, verses, and metaphors. But he is also the strong poet who has absolute control over them. He uses metres, verses, and metaphors to produce the music which you cannot but admire. He governs from above but does not dictate" (ibid.).

The instruments of his control are, of course, defined in dharmic, and at the individual level, sva-dharmic terms. And therein, I think, arises the problem for us. Such a view assumes a whole social hierarchy where permitted actions are predefined in accordance with a real or notional consensus about what actions are appropriate or ethical for particular categories of people (spelt out, for instance, in the last chapter of the *Gītā* itself; see 18.41-47). What counts as correct or moral action *in the world* is not argued for in the *Gītā*; it is assumed by it. But most of us, for instance do not — perhaps cannot — make the same assumptions. What constitutes our duty in the modern world is seldom predefined or taken for granted, and the *Gītā* does not help us with this.

So the question arises of how the *Gītā's* world- or karma-transcending ethic of non-attachment might work outside the context of a pre-established, (sva-)dharmic worldview. It seems to me that this depends upon coming to an agreement to our own satisfaction about the nature of moral action *in the world.* There is then no reason why we should not, if we so wish, employ the *Gita*'s method of world-transcending and world-transforming internal renunciation as a means to freedom. That, after all, is its *raison d'etre.* I would suggest, however, that to employ the *Gītā's* soteriological method — the giving up of the fruits of our actions to God — without such a pre-established "worldly" moral framework, would present all kinds of practical and ethical problems, and, therefore, that method could hardly function on its own as a guide to living in the world. Acting without *attachment* to the results of one's actions comes perilously close to acting without *regard* for the results of one's actions, unless an agreed moral framework is already in place. In the *Gītā,* of course, there *is* such a framework, and it has been validated by God.

1 See R Gombrich, 1988, and P Olivelle, 1992, for discussions of this general problem in its historical context.

2 See the Introduction to my translation of the *Gītā* (1994), pp.x-xviii, for an overview of the social and historical context.

3 All translations of passages from the *Gītā* are taken from my 1994 translation.

4 P Olivelle, 1993: 105.

5 As Arvind Sharma has written, "Both the theistic and absolutistic traditions lay claim to the Gītā later as a bright jewel in their own crown!", 1986: 14.

6 Paul Hacker used this term "inclusivism" ("Inclusivismus"). See W Halbfass, 1988: 403-18 for a discussion.

7 See, for instance, A Sharma on the "gnostic rather than *bhakti* orientation of the *Anugītā*" (op.cit.,p.6), where a tendentious re-reading or re-editing of the *Gītā* results in its "fruits of *bhakti*" being offered as the *Anugītā's* "fruits of *jñāna*" (p.7).

8 This raises two related questions, which cannot be considered in detail here: 1) what kind of text is the *Gītā*?, and 2) how should we read it? As I have said, it is just as possible to make a case for an Advaitin or monistic interpretation of the *Gītā*, as it is for a monotheistic interpretation. Such variety is obtained by selective and mutually incompatible readings of the text, which in the modern period share an underlying assumption that the *Gītā* is chronologically and editorially layered, the product of various hands at various times. To take just one example: A L Basham (1990: 82-97) argues that the text is the work of at least three different hands, each propounding a different soteriological path. That is to say, he evaluates the *Gītā* as one would a literary, or series of literary compositions, highlighting its apparent inconsistencies. This, however, seems to beg the question of just how the *Gītā* was transmitted up to the point we can be sure of a settled text (i.e. the one commented upon by Śaṃkara).
It may be the case that what seem to be irreconcilable inconsistencies in a written and carefully studied text (i.e. a literary composition) disappear when that text is viewed as the product of an oral tradition. For example, Basham's remark that "no one of sound mind could have composed verses 23 to 28 of the fifth chapter of the *Bhagavad-gītā* and then negated them as an afterthought with verse 29" (op.cit., p.86), only applies if one has decided on evidence other than that provided by the text itself that verses 5.23-28, and verse 5.29, refer to two discrete and fully developed religio-philosophical systems. It would perhaps be more fruitful, as well as more faithful to the nature of the text as an originally oral construct, to treat such "inconsistencies" in the light of the *Gītā's* overriding soteriological principle of *bhakti*. Rather than irreconcilable, such verses then become exemplars of the layering and hierarchising process so typical of orally transmitted accounts and of Indian religious culture in general. In other words, one element is *added* to another, not opposed to it, thereby increasing the overall religious and dramatic effect. It is on this reading of the *Gītā*, as a reflective but not literary construction, that I base my current discussion of its soteriology. That is to say, I am commenting on the text we have (the compiler's text, if that is what it is) *as a whole*. I do not assume that it is two, three, or any other number of different texts. Whether that whole text is the result of editorial manipulation, or evidence of a consistent theological position, or something else, we cannot know with certainty. But to get beyond the form of the text to its contents, we have to assume at least self-containment, if not total internal coherence — an assumption made by its classical commentators and the Hindu tradition in general. On the *Gītā's* "multivalency", see A Sharma, op.cit., Introduction and Conclusion.

9 R Gombrich, 1981: 996.

10 R C Zaehner, 1966: 106-7.

11 J D Smith, in A T Hatto (ed.), 1980: 71-2.

12 My translation of: *kṛtaḥ puruṣkāraḥ sanso'pi daivena sidhyati/ tathāsya karmaṇaḥ kartur abhinivartate phalam//* 10.2.10.

13 A distinction made by Gombrich, op.cit., p.995.

14 This returns us to the question of how we should read the *Gītā*. In particular, the question arises of whether attribution of total agency to Krishna is intended to be read in a literal or just a laudatory sense. If the latter is intended, then the problem of free will is not even raised, let alone confronted. Knowledge is only important for the devotee in so far as it engenders an attitude which results in devotion. The question of who is the real agent is more crucial where knowledge alone, i.e. knowledge of the way things really are, is regarded as the path to liberation. But as we have seen, in the *Gītā* the overriding relationship is of knowledge at the service of *bhakti*. The question of whether what the knower knows is literally true or merely instrumental (it might be both, of course) is not directly addressed. This leaves an ambiguity concerning the identity of the true agent, but perhaps a necessary one, given the *Gītā's* synthetic role and its attempt to forge a compromise. On the question of Krishna's universal agency, Professor Humphrey Palmer has pointed out to me in a personal communication that much Christian piety refers to, and even yearns for, God's total takeover of the individual, but the devotee's actions and other conversation show that this is not meant literally.

15 Here I am not considering the idea, secondary to the text itself, that simply by listening to the *Gītā* one may be liberated, or as Sharma puts it, "It.....sacralises by its mere recitation", op.cit., p.15. See also Sharma on the *Gītā* offering "several optional paths to salvation" (p.254ff).

16 Rather than simply as an anthology of "alternate ways of attaining the supreme end" (A Sharma, op.cit., p.252).

17 Similarly, although as Basham says, "The text lays much emphasis, as do some Upanishads, on the last state of mind of a dying person as promoting salvation" (op.cit., pp.92-3), this idea too is subsumed under *bhakti* (i.e. devotion to Krishna) in the *Gītā* (see 8.5).

18 W Halbfass, 1988: 336.

19 B K Matilal, 1989: 18.

Glossary[1]

agapé: altruistic love.

ahaṃkāra: the sense of self; the ego.

apavarga: the final goal; liberation from rebirth.

artha: (i) meaning; (ii) object, wealth (one of the "puruṣārthas").

āśrama: one of four stages of life (that of being a student, or householder, or forest-recluse, or renouncer).

avatāra: "descent" of heavenly individual(s), usually the deity, into embodied form.

Bhagavān: the deity as one's object of devotion; the Lord.

bhakta: a devotee.

bhakti: loving devotion.

Brahmin: priest/priestly order of the "caste" system.

caritas: love, friendship.

caturvarga: "the group of four": dharma, kāma, artha, mokṣa (see "trivarga").

dharma: code of conduct; righteousness (one of the "puruṣārthas").

eros: self-centred, gratifying, love.

ghee: clarified butter.

1 This Glossary is not exhaustive of all the Sanskrit terms used in this book.

gṛhastha: householder, one who iṣ in the second āśrama.

guṇa: (i) quality; (ii) a constituent of "prakṛti", either "sattva", "rajas" or "tamas".

jñāna: knowledge.

jñānī: possessor of knowledge; an enlightened person (masculine noun).

kāma: desire, pleasure, gratification (one of the "puruṣārthas").

karma: in conjunction with "rebirth" the metaphysical residue of self-centred actions, which leads to transmigration.

karmabhūmi: field of action.

karman: action (traditionally, ritual action).

kartā (kartṛ): an agent; one who performs an action.

kratvartha: "for the sake of the (sacrificial, not one's personal) intention."

Kṣatriya: warrior; member of the second or ruling order of the "caste" system.

līlā: "play", i.e. spontaneous or non-calculating activity.

māyā: (i) dazzling display; (ii) illusion.

mokṣa: liberation from rebirth (one of the "puruṣārthas").

nirguṇa: without characteristics (see "saguṇa").

nirvāṇa: an indescribable state of enlightenment and liberation from the cycle of rebirth.

nivṛtti: attitude/practice of withdrawal from the world.

Om: mystic syllable.

pāda: "foot" or part of a verse.

prakṛti: (i) "Nature"; (ii) the principle of space and time in Sāṃkhya philosophy.

pralaya: dissolution (of the world).

pravṛtti: attitude/practice of engagement with the world.

puruṣa: (i) (male) person; (ii) the spiritual principle in Sāṃkhya philosophy.

puruṣārtha: goals of human living (see "caturvarga").

rajas: one of the three "guṇas" of "prakṛti" (ii), responsible for such characteristics as motion, speed, aggression, passion.

saguṇa: with characteristics (see nirguṇa).

Saṃhitā: "collection", especially of Vedic verses.

saṃkalpa: resolve, intention to perform an action.

saṃnyāsa: practice of renunciation.

saṃnyāsin: renouncer.

saṃsāra: the stream of life, of the cycle of birth, death and rebirth.

saṃskāra: purifying, perfecting rite of passage.

Śāstra: authoritative text.

sattva: one of the three "guṇas" of "prakṛti" (ii), responsible for such characteristics as lightness, brightness, intelligence, health and serenity.

śloka: a kind of metrical verse.

smṛti: "remembering", i.e. authoritative tradition.

Soma: a plant used by the Vedic Indians for sacrificial purposes; the heady juice of this plant.

Śramaṇa: renouncer-ascetic (especially Buddhists and Jains).

śruti: "the hearing", i.e. canonical scripture (=Veda).

strī-dharma: the dharma prescribed for women.

Śūdra: member of the fourth and lowest order of the "caste" system, whose duty it is to attend to the top three orders.

sva-dharma: one's own dharma; the dharma prescribed for oneself.

tamas: one of the three "guṇas" of "prakṛti" (ii), responsible for such characteristics as inertia, dullness, sloth, and stupidity.

tapas: ascetic power.

tattva: truth; principle/category of being.

trivarga: "the group of three", i.e. dharma, kāma, and artha (see "caturvarga").

Vaiśya: trader, member of the third order of the "caste" system.

varṇa: one of the four basic caste-orders (Brahmin, Kṣatriya, Vaiśya, Śūdra).

Veda: canonical scriptural knowledge (= śruti).

vidhi: (Vedic) injunction.

yoga: any integrative discipline.

yuga: mythic eon of time.

Bibliography

Āpastamba, *Āpastamba Dharmasūtra with the Commentary Ujjwala by Sri Haradatta Misra,* edited by A. Chinnaswami Sastri and A.R. Sastri, Kashi Sanskrit Series, No. 93, Benares, 1932.

Baijnath, Rai Bahadur Lala, *The Bhagavadgita in Modern Life,* Vaishya Hitkari, Meerut, 1908.

Bailey, G, "Suffering in the Mahābhārata: Draupadī and Yudhiṣṭhira", in *Puruṣārtha* 7, 1983.

Bailey, G, "On D D Kosambi's interpretation of the Bhagavadgītā", in *Indologica Taurinensia* 12, 1984.

Basham, A L, *The Sacred Cow: the Evolution of Classical Hinduism,* Rider ed., London etc., 1990.

Bazaz, Prem N, *The Role of Bhagavad Gita in Indian History,* Sterling Publishers, New Delhi, 1975.

Bhaktivedanta Swami, AC, *The Science of Self-Realization,* Bhkativedanta Book Trust, London, 1977.

Bhargava, P Lal, "Additions and Interpolations in the *Bhagavadgītā*", in *East and West (NS),* 27, 1977.

Biardeau, M, "Études de mythologie hindoue", pt.3, in *Bulletin de l'École Française d'Éxtrême — Orient* 58, 1971.

Biardeau, M, *Hinduism: The Anthropology of a Civilization* (ET), Oxford University Press, Delhi, 1989.

Brockington, J L, *Righteous Rāma: the Evolution of an Epic,* Oxford University Press, Delhi, 1984.

Brown, J, *Gandhi: prisoner of hope,* Yale University Press, New Haven, 1989.

Butler, C, *The Theology of Vatican II,* Darton, Longman and Todd, London, 1967.

Chatterjee, M, *Gandhi's Religious Thought,* Macmillan, Basingstoke, 1983.

Clooney, F X, *Thinking Ritually: Rediscovering the Pūrva Mīmāṃsā of Jaimini,* De Nobili Research Library, Vienna, 1990.

Dayānanda Sarasvatī, *Introduction to the Vedic Commentary (Ṛg-vedādi-bhūmikā),* trans. Ghasi Ram, Arya Pratinidhi Sabha, 1925.

de Nicolas, A, *The Bhagavad Gita,* Nicolas-Hays Inc., York Beach, Maine, 1990.

Deshpande, Madhav M, "The Epic Context of the *Bhagavadgītā*", in A Sharma (ed.), *Essays on the Mahābhārata,* E J Brill, Leiden, 1991.

De Smet, R V, "The Gītā in time and beyond time", in *The Bhagavad Gita and the Bible,* SPCK, Unity Books, Delhi, 1975.

De Smet, R V, "A Copernican Reversal: the Gītākāra's reformulation of karma", in *Philosophy East and West* 27, 1977.

Dhavamony, M, *The Love of God according to Śaiva Siddhānta,* Clarendon Press, Oxford, 1971.

D'Sa, F X, "Dharma as delight in cosmic welfare: a study of dharma in the Gita", in *Bible Bhashyam* 6.4, 1980.

Eder, M, "A Review of Recent *Bhagavadgītā* Studies", in *Journal of South Asian Literature,* 23.2, 1988.

Edgerton, F, *The Bhagavad Gītā,* vol.II, Harvard University Press, Cambridge, Mass., 1944.

Emeneau, M B, "*Bhagavadgītā* Notes", in *Mélanges d'Indianisme à la mémoire de Louis Renou,* Éditions E de Boccard, Paris, 1968.

Esnoul, A-M (trans.), *Nārāyaṇīya Parvan du Mahābhārata,* Société d'Édition "Les Belles Lettres", Paris, 1979.

Galbraith, J, *The New Industrial State,* Houghton Mifflin, Boston, 1979.

Gandhi, M K, *MK Gandhi interprets the Bhagavadgita,* Orient Paperbacks, Delhi, n.d.

Gautama, *The Gautama Dharma Sūtra with the Mitākṣarā Sanskrit Commentary of Haradatta,* edited by U.C. Pandey, Kashi Sanskrit Series, No. 172, Varanasi, 1966.

Glucklich, A, *Religious Jurisprudence in the Dharmaśāstras,* Macmillan, New York, 1988.

Glucklich, A, *The Sense of Adharma,* Oxford University Press, Oxford, 1994.

Gombrich, R, "On pain of retribution", *Times Literary Supplement,* September 4, 1981.

Gombrich, R, *Theravāda Buddhism: A social history from ancient Benares to modern Colombo,* Routledge and Kegan Paul, London and New York, 1988.

Gonda, J, *Change and Continuity in Indian Religion,* Mouton, the Hague, 1965.

Gopal, S, *Radhakrishnan: a biography,* Oxford University Press, Delhi, 1989.

Hacker, P, "Schopenhauer und die Ethik des Hinduismus", *Saeculum* 4, 1961, trans. into English by D Killingley in W Halbfass (1995), see below.

Halbfass, W, *India and Europe: An Essay in Understanding,* State University of New York Press, Albany, 1988.

Halbfass, W (ed.), *Philology and Confrontation: Paul Hacker on Traditional and Modern Vedanta,* State University of New York Press, Albany, 1995.

Heesterman, J, *The Inner Conflict of Tradition: Essays in Indian Ritual, Kingship, and Society,* Chicago University Press, Chicago, 1985.

Hiltebeitel, Alf, *The Ritual of Battle: Krishna in the* Mahābhārata, Cornell University Press, Ithaca, 1976.

Hiltebeitel, Alf, "The two Kṛṣṇas on one chariot: Upaniṣadic imagery and Epic mythology", in *History of Religions,* 24, 1984-5.

Hiryanna, M, *The Quest after Perfection,* Kavyalaya Publishers, Mysore, 1952.

Ingalls, D, "Dharma and Mokṣa" in *Philosophy East and West* 7, 1957-8.

Jacobi, H, "Über die Einfügung der Bhagavadgītā im Mahābhārata", in *Zeitschrift der Deutschen Morgenländischen Gesellschaft* 72, 1918.

Jeźic, M, "The first Yoga layer in the *Bhagavadgītā*", in *Ludwik Sternbach Felicitation Volume,* Akhila Bharatiya Sanskrit Parishad, Lucknow, 1979.

Jeźic, M, "Textual Layers of the *Bhagavadgītā* as traces of Indian cultural history", in *Sanskrit and World Culture: Proceedings of the Fourth World Sanskrit Conference,* Akademie-Verlag, Berlin, 1986.

Johnson, W J, *The Bhagavad Gita,* Oxford University Press, Oxford, 1994.

Johnston, E H, *Early Sāṃkhya,* Royal Asiatic Society, London, 1937.

Kane, P V, *History of Dharmaśāstra,* Bhandarkar Oriental Institute, Poona, 1977.

Kauṭilya, *The Kauṭilīya Arthaśāstra in 3 Parts,* Part I: the Sanskrit text, 1960; Part II: Translation with Notes, 1963; Part III: A Study, 1965, by R.P. Kangle, University of Bombay, Bombay, 1960-65.

Keynes, G, (editor), *Blake. Complete Writings,* Oxford University Press, 1972.

Khair, G S, *Quest for the Original Gītā,* Somaiya Publications, Bombay, 1969.

Klaes, N, *Conscience and Consciousness: Ethical Problems of the Mahābhārata,* Dharmaram College, Bangalore, 1975.

Kosambi, D D, "Social and economic aspects of the Bhagavad Gītā", in *Journal of the Economic and Social History of the Orient* 4, 1961.

Krishna, Daya, *Indian Philosophy, A Counter Perspective,* Oxford University Press, Delhi, 1991.

Lipner, J, "Applying the litmus test: a comparative study in Vedantic exegesis", in J Lipner (ed.) and D Killingley (asst.ed.), *A Net Cast Wide: Investigations into Indian Thought in Memory of David Friedman,* Grevatt & Grevatt, Newcastle upon Tyne, 1986.

Lipner, J, *Hindus: Their Religious Beliefs and Practices,* Routledge, London, 1994.

Malamoud, C, "On the Rhetoric and Semantics of the Puruṣārthas", in T N Madan (ed.), *Way of Life: King, Householder, Renouncer,* Motilal Banarsidass, Delhi, 1988.

Manu, *Manusmṛti with the Sanskrit Commentary Manvarthamuktāvalī of Kullūka Bhaṭṭa,* edited by J.L. Shastri, Motilal Banarsidass, Delhi, 1983.

Mascaro, J, *The Bhagavad Gita,* Penguin Books, London, 1962.

Mascaro, J, *The Upanishads,* Penguin Classics, London, 1965.

Matilal, B K (ed.), *Moral Dilemmas in the Mahābhārata,* Indian Institute of Advanced Study, Shimla, 1989.

McElvaney M, in Y Williams and M McElvaney (eds.), *Aurobindo and Zaehner on the Bhagavad-Gītā,* STIMW Series 1, S Y Killingley, Newcastle upon Tyne, 1988.

Minor, R N, "The *Gītā's* Way as the Only Way", in *Philosophy East and West* 30.3, 1980.

Minor, R N, *Bhagavad-Gītā: an exegetical commentary,* Heritage Publishers, New Delhi/South Asia Books, Columbia, Missouri, 1982.

Minor, R N, *Modern Interpreters of the Bhagavad Gītā,* State University of New York Press, Albany, 1986.

Neufeldt, R W, "A Lesson in Allegory: Theosophical Interpretations of the *Bhagavadgītā*", in R N Minor (1986) above.

Norman, K R, *The Rhinoceros Horn and Other Early Buddhist Poems*, Pali Text Society, London, 1985.

Oberlies, T, "Die Śvetāśvatara Upaniṣad: eine Studie ihrer Gotteslehre", in *Wiener Zeitschrift für die Kunde Südasiens und Archiv für indische Philosophie* 32, 1988.

Oberlies, T, "Die Śvetāśvatara Upaniṣad: Einleitung — Edition und Übersetzung von Adhyāya 1", in *Wiener Zeitschrift für die Kunde Südasiens und Archiv für indische Philosophie* 39, 1995.

O'Connor, G, *The Mahābhārata: Peter Brook's epic in the making*, Hodder and Stoughton, London, 1989.

O'Flaherty, W D, *The Rig Veda, An Anthology*, Penguin Books, London, 1981.

Olivelle, P, *Saṃnyāsa Upaniṣads: Hindu Scriptures on Asceticism and Renunciation*, Oxford University Press, New York, 1992.

Olivelle, P, *The Āśrama System: the History and Hermeneutics of Religious Institution*, Oxford University Press, Oxford, 1993.

Oltramare, P, "Le Mahabharata, témoin du conflit de la tradition et de l'esprit nouveau", in *Actes du Congrès International d'Histoire des Religions, Paris, 1923;* vol.2, Librairie Ancienne Honoré Champion, Paris, 1925.

Oltramare, P, "La *Bhagavad-Gītā*, partie intégrante du *Mahābhārata*", in *Revue de l'histoire de religions*, 97, 1928.

Otto, R, *Die Urgestalt der Bhagavad-Gītā*, J C B Mohr, Tübingen, 1934.

Otto, R, *Die Lehrtraktate der Bhagavad-Gītā*, J C B Mohr, Tübingen, 1935.

Panikkar, R, *The Vedic Experience. Mantramañjarī. An Anthology of the Vedas for Modern Man and Contemporary Celebration*, Darton, Longman and Todd, London, 1977.

Pollock, Sheldon, "Deep Orientalism?", in C A Breckenridge and P van der Veer (eds.), *Orientalism and the Postcolonial Predicament: Perspectives on South Asia*, University of Pennsylvania Press, 1993.

Potter, K, *Presuppositions of India's Philosophies*, Motilal Banarsidass, Delhi, 1991 (first published under same title by Prentice-Hall, Englewood Cliffs, 1963).

Prabhupada, AC Bhaktivedanta Swami, *The Bhagavad Gita as it is*, Bhaktivedanta Book Trust, Letchmore Heath, reprint of 1968 ed.(See also under Bhaktivedanta Swami).

Radhakrishnan, S, *The Bhagavadgītā with an introductory essay, Sanskrit text, English translation and notes*, 2nd ed., George Allen and Unwin, London, 1949.

Radhakrishnan, S, *The Principal Upaniṣads*, George Allen and Unwin, London, 1953.

Renou, L, *Prolégomènes au Vedānta par Śaṅkara*, Adrien-Maisonneuve, Paris, 1951.

Robinson, J, *Economic Philosophy*, C A Watts and Co., London, 1962.

Robinson, J, *The Accumulation of Capital*, Macmillan, New York, 1965.

Routley, E, *Hymns and Human Life*, John Murray, London, 1952.

Ruben, W, *Krishna: Konkordanz und Kommentar der Motive seines Heldenlebens*, n.p., Istanbul, 1944.

Sachse, J, *Ze studiów nad Bhagavadgītā*, Acta Universitatis Wratislaviensis 1038, Wydawnictwo

Uniwersytetu Wroclawskiego, Wroclaw, 1988.

Sadhale, G S, *The Bhagavad-Gita with Eleven Commentaries,* 2nd ed., Gujarati Printing Press, Bombay, 1935.

Samuelson, P, *Economics,* Mc-Graw Hill, New York, 1976.

Sargeant, W, *The Bhagavad Gītā,* revd. ed., State University of New York Press, Albany, 1994.

Sastry, A Mahadeva, *The Bhagavad Gita with the commentary of Sri Sankaracharya,* Samata Books, Madras, 1979, reprint of 1901 ed.

Shankar, A, *Warning: India in danger,* Vishwa Hindu Parishad Pamphlet, Leicester, n.d.

Sharma, A, *The Puruṣārthas: A Study in Hindu Axiology,* Asian Studies Center, Michigan State University, East Lansing, 1982.

Sharma, A, *The Hindu Gītā: Ancient and Classical Interpretations of the Bhagavadgītā,* Duckworth, 1986.

Smith, J D, "Old Indian: The Two Sanskrit Epics", in A T Hatto (ed.), *Traditions of Heroic and Epic Poetry, vol.1: The Traditions,* Modern Humanities Research Association, London, 1980.

Smith, J D, "Scapegoats of the Gods: the Ideology of the Indian Epics", in S H Blackburn et al. (eds.), *Oral Epics in India,* University of California Press, Berkeley, 1989.

Smith, R Morton, "Statistics of the Bhagavadgītā", in *Journal of the Ganganath Jha Research Institute,* 24, 1968.

Stevenson, R, "Tilak and the *Bhagavadgītā's* Doctrine of Karmayoga", in R N Minor (1986) above.

Thapar, R, *Interpreting Early India,* Oxford University Press, Oxford, 1993.

Tilak, B G, *Gitarahasya or Karmayoga,* 4th English ed., DJ Tilak and SS Tilak, trans. from the Marathi by A S Sukthankar, Poona, 1980.

Tracy, D, "The Return of God in Contemporary Theology", in Geffré, C, and Jeanrond, W, (editors), *Why Theology?* issue of *Concilium,* 1994/6.

van Buitenen, J A B, "A Contribution to the Critical Edition of the Bhagavadgītā", in *Journal of the American Oriental Society* 85, 1965.

van Buitenen, J A B, *Rāmānuja on the Bhagavadgītā,* 2nd ed., Motilal Banarsidass, Delhi, 1968.

van Buitenen, J A B, *The Bhagavadgītā in the Mahābhārata,* Chicago University Press, Chicago, 1981.

Vātsyāyana, *The Kāmasūtra with the Commentary Jayamaṅgala of Yashodhar,* edited by Gosvami Damodhar Shastri, Kashi Sanskrit Series, No. 29, Benares, 1929.

von Simson, G, "Die Einschaltung der *Bhagavadgītā* im *Bhīṣmaparvan* des *Mahābhārata*", in *Indo-Iranian Journal,* 11, 1969.

Whittier, J G, *Poetical Works,* Cambridge, Massachusetts, 1895.

Wilfred, F, *From the Dusty Soil,* University of Madras, Madras, 1995.

Williams, D (ed.), *Peter Brook and the Mahābhārata: critical perspectives,* Routledge, London,1991

Yājñavalkya, *Yājñavalkyasmṛti of Yogīshwara Yājñavalkya with the Mitākṣarā Commentary of Vijñāneshwar,* edited by U.C. Pandey, Kashi Sanskrit Series, No. 178, Varanasi, 1967.

Yardi, M R, *The Bhagavadgītā as a Synthesis,* Bhandarkar Oriental Series, 25, Bhandarkar Oriental

Research Institute, Poona, 1991.

Zaehner, R C, *Hinduism,* Oxford University Press, Oxford, 1962, 1966.

Zaehner, R C, "'Standing on the Peak', a concept common to the Bhagavad-Gītā and the Victorines", in *Studies in Mysticism and Religion presented to G G Scholem,* Hebrew University, Jerusalem, 1967.

Zaehner, R C, *The Bhagavad Gītā,* Clarendon Press, Oxford, 1969.

Zelliot, E, *From Untouchable to Dalit: essays on the Ambedkar movement,* Manohar, New Delhi, 1992.

Notes on Contributors

John Brockington is Reader in and Head of the Department of Sanskrit at the University of Edinburgh. Besides numerous articles for various journals, he has written an introduction to Hinduism, *The Sacred Thread: Hinduism in its Continuity and Diversity* (The University Press, Edinburgh, 1981), a study of the *Rāmāyaṇa* of Vālmīki, *Righteous Rāma* (Oxford University Press, Delhi, 1984), and a work in the comparative study of religion, *Hinduism and Christianity: Themes in Comparative Religion* (Macmillan, London, 1992). His special area of research is the Sanskrit epics, and he is Convenor of the "Ritual and Devotion" Working Group of DHIIR (the Dharam Hinduja Institute of Indic Research) at Cambridge, as well as a member of its Advisory Council.

Gavin Flood teaches Indian Religions in the Theology and Religious Studies Department of the University of Wales at Lampeter. His publications include *Body and Cosmology in Kashmir Śaivism* (Mellen Research University Press, San Francisco, 1993), *An Introduction to Hinduism* (Cambridge University Press, 1996), and articles in books and periodicals. He is doing research on Kashmir Śaivism, the tantric traditions of Kerala, ritual, and Religious Studies Methodology. Dr Flood is Convenor of the "Challenges to the Veda" Working Group of DHIIR at Cambridge.

Ashis Gupta is Professor in the Faculty of Management at the University of Calgary in Canada. His early studies were in India, after which he took a doctorate in English Literature from Boston University and continued postdoctoral studies at Harvard University and the Massachusetts Institute of Technology. He has lectured and published widely on the way culture and environment influence business management. Professor Gupta has also written several novels.

Jacqueline Suthren Hirst is lecturer in Comparative Religion at the Department of Religions and Theology at the University of Manchester, where she specialises in Indian Religions. Before she went to Manchester she was Senior Lecturer in Religious Studies at Homerton College for the training of teachers at the University of Cambridge. Her research interests and publications have focused on the Advaitic tradition and especially on Śaṃkara, on whom she got her PhD in the Divinity Faculty at Cambridge and is now completing a book. Dr Hirst is a member of the "Dharma and Gender" Working Group of DHIIR (Cambridge).

Will Johnson was educated at the University of Sussex and Wolfson College, Oxford, where he was Michael Coulson Research Fellow in Indology from 1991 to 1992. He now lectures at the University of Wales, Cardiff, where he teaches classical Indian Religions and Sanskrit. A book based on his doctoral thesis, and entitled *Harmless Souls: Karmic Bondage and Religious Change in Early Jainism* has recently been published (Motilal Banarsidass, Delhi, 1995), and his translation of the *Bhagavadgītā* for Oxford University Press's World's Classics Series appeared in 1994. He is currently working on a translation of the *Sauptikaparvan* of the *Mahābhārata* for the same Series, and a book on Jainism and the religious arts. Dr Johnson is a member of the "Challenges to the Veda" Working Group of DHIIR at Cambridge.

Dermot Killingley is Senior Lecturer in the Department of Religious Studies at the University of Newcastle upon Tyne where he runs an annual Seminar on the Sanskrit Tradition in the Modern World. In 1990 he gave the Westcott Memorial Lectures (more commonly known as the Teape Lectures) in Bangalore, Calcutta and Delhi.

His publications include *Rammohun Roy in Hindu and Christian Tradition* (his Teape Lectures, published by Grevatt & Grevatt, Newcastle upon Tyne, 1993), and with W Menski and S Firth, *Hindu Ritual and Society* (Grevatt & Grevatt, Newcastle upon Tyne, 1991). He has also written, with Robert Jackson, a book for teachers, *Approaches to Hinduism* (John Murray, London, 1988); he has published widely in learned journals, and is working on a Sanskrit teaching book. Dr Killingley is Convenor of the ""Veda' and its Forms" Working Group of DHIIR (Cambridge).

Nicholas Lash is Norris Hulse Professor of Divinity at Cambridge. He has published and lectured widely. His publications include, *A Matter of Hope. A Theologian's Reflections on the Thought of Karl Marx* (Darton, Longman & Todd, London, 1981), and *Easter in Ordinary. Reflections on Human Experience and the Knowledge of God* (SCM Press, London, 1988). In 1994, after a period of nearly fifty years, he returned to India, where he was born, to give the Teape Lectures on Hindu and Christian thought, which have been included in a recent book of his: *The Beginning and the End of "Religion"* (Cambridge University Press, 1996).

Julius Lipner lectures in Indian religion and in the comparative study of religion at the Divinity Faculty in Cambridge, and is Director of DHIIR. Of Indian extraction, he was born and raised in India. His publications include *The Face of Truth: A Study of Meaning and Metaphysics in the Vedantic Theology of Rāmānuja* (Macmillan, London, & SUNY, Albany, 1986), and *Hindus: their religious beliefs and practices* (Routledge, London, 1994). At present he is completing a book on the life and thought of the Bengali religious thinker and nationalist, Brahmabandhab Upadhyay (1861-1907).

Index